Vintage Campers,

TRAILERS, AND TEARDROPS

Quarto.com

© 2024 Quarto Publishing Group USA Inc.
Text © 2021 Patrick R. Foster

Paperback edition published in 2024

First Published in 2021 by Motorbooks, an imprint of The Quarto Group,
100 Cummings Center, Suite 265-D, Beverly, MA 01915, USA.
T (978) 282-9590 F (978) 283-2742

All rights reserved. No part of this book may be reproduced in any form without written permission of the copyright owners. All images in this book have been reproduced with the knowledge and prior consent of the artists concerned, and no responsibility is accepted by producer, publisher, or printer for any infringement of copyright or otherwise, arising from the contents of this publication. Every effort has been made to ensure that credits accurately comply with information supplied. We apologize for any inaccuracies that may have occurred and will resolve inaccurate or missing information in a subsequent reprinting of the book.

Motorbooks titles are also available at discount for retail, wholesale, promotional, and bulk purchase. For details, contact the Special Sales Manager by email at specialsales@quarto.com or by mail at The Quarto Group, Attn: Special Sales Manager, 100 Cummings Center, Suite 265-D, Beverly, MA 01915, USA.

ISBN: 978-0-7603-9739-8

Digital edition published in 2021
eISBN: 978-0-7603-6682-0

Library of Congress Cataloging-in-Publication Data

Names: Foster, Patrick R., author.
Title: Vintage campers, trailers and teardrops / by Patrick R. Foster.
Description: Beverly, MA, USA : Motorbooks, an imprint of The Quarto Group, 2020. | Includes bibliographical references and index. | Summary: "Vintage Campers, Trailers & Teardrops is an entertaining photographic history of classic camper culture and travel from the 1930s to the present"-- Provided by publisher.
Identifiers: LCCN 2020006694 | ISBN 9780760366813 (hardcover) | ISBN 9780760366820 (ebook)
Subjects: LCSH: Truck campers--United States--History. | Camping trailers--United States--History.
Classification: LCC TL298 .F67 2020 | DDC 629.2260973--dc23
LC record available at https://lccn.loc.gov/2020006694

Acquiring Editor: Dennis Pernu
Art Director: Cindy Samargia Laun
Cover and Page Design: Simon Larkin
Cover Image: Classic Stock/Alamy Stock Photo

Vintage Campers,
TRAILERS, AND TEARDROPS

PATRICK R. FOSTER

Contents

CHAPTER ONE – 6
VINTAGE CAMPING
WHY IS THIS HOBBY GROWING SO QUICKLY? BECAUSE IT'S A TREMENDOUS AMOUNT OF FUN!

CHAPTER TWO – 28
TIN CANS, CANNED HAMS, WOODEN TEARDROPS, AND CAMPER TRAILERS
PERHAPS THE MOST SOUGHT-AFTER VINTAGE CAMPERS.

CHAPTER THREE – 50
FROM COVERED WAGONS TO . . . COVERED WAGONS
THE HISTORY OF CAMPERS AND ONE OF THE MOST ICONIC BRANDS.

CHAPTER FOUR – 64
PICKUP SHELLS AND SLIDE-IN CAMPERS
THE SUBHOBBY OF CAMPER SHELLS. HERE'S WHAT YOU NEED TO KNOW.

CHAPTER FIVE – 82
VINTAGE EUROPEAN CAMPING AND THE VW PHENOMENON
BRITS AND GERMANS ARE ESPECIALLY BIG FANS OF "CARAVANNING."

CHAPTER SIX – 106
THE VINTAGE CAMPER LIFE
IT'S A WAY OF LIFE FOR SOME. HERE'S HOW TO ENJOY THIS HOBBY TO THE FULLEST.

CHAPTER SEVEN – 120
SILVER BULLETS: THE AIRSTREAM STORY
AN ENTIRE CHAPTER ON AIRSTREAM? EVERYBODY LOVES AIRSTREAMS!

CHAPTER EIGHT – 146
POP-UP TRAILERS
THE BEGINNER'S SEGMENT OF THE MARKET. HERE ARE THE POPULAR BRANDS.

ACKNOWLEDGMENTS – 158
IMAGE CREDITS – 158
ABOUT THE AUTHOR – 158
INDEX – 159

Nothing illustrates the fun and beauty of vintage campers better than a true classic like this 1960 Holiday House Model 19. The curved kitchen windows and bright chrome exterior, accented with red inside and out, make this a highly desirable collector vehicle. Finding one may prove difficult, as fewer than 200 were produced.

CHAPTER ONE

Vintage Camping

On vacation. Unavailable. Away for the week. Gone. Are there any sweeter words in the English language? It's a fact: everybody needs to get away from it all now and then, to clear the brain, recharge the batteries, to just feel free for a change. And for millions of people around the world, the best way to do that is to hook a camper or trailer to the back of the family vehicle and head out. To freedom and the great outdoors. To live!

This luxury trailer, circa 1926, has large windows for a bright, airy feeling and plenty of interior room. Notice the side door curves into the roofline to allow plenty of room for entry and exit.

And that's really what it's all about, isn't it? To live life to the fullest, to get the most pleasure out of each day, any way we can. Life should be an adventure, and travel is one of the best paths to adventure. There's just something about taking your home with you—stopping wherever you want to, being in the comfort of your own abode and able to cook your own meals while away—that really appeals to people. Camping is one of the most popular ways to get away from it all, a tradition enjoyed by people around the globe. And enthusiasts are divided equally between men and women.

VINTAGE CAMPING

The fastest growing segment of the camping craze is camping out in a vintage camper, trailer, fifth wheel, slide-in, or pop-up. It's a cool way to travel. When you're trucking down the highway with your vintage camper in tow or all set up in a campground with your vintage Airstream, Shasta, or Holiday Rambler, you're the one that everybody wishes they were, seemingly just a bit more special than everyone else. Okay, we'll say it—you rule!

Just how popular is vintage camping? Well, Instagram has more than 4.5 million posts with the hashtag #vanlife! An online search for the term "vintage camper" on Airbnb turns up with a whopping 90,000 entries. That's a lot of rental opportunities if you're looking to give it a try before you buy.

There are lots of vintage camper clubs to join too. As just one example, the website for Vintage Camper Trailers has two groups: Tow Boyz and Tow Girlz. They cost nothing to join and there are no dues or fees involved, but they do offer a pretty useful website (www.vintagecampertrailers.com) and publish a good magazine targeting vintage camper enthusiasts. Lots of other resources are also included later in the book.

For a more classic 1940s look, try a classic breadbox-style camper like this 1948 Alma, which was built in Alma, Michigan. It's roomy, stylish, and sure to attract attention wherever you go.

This cartoon says it all; wherever you roam in your vintage camper, you're always at home. You sleep in your own bed, eat in your own kitchen, go in your own toile… well, you get the idea.

SO, WHO GOES CAMPING?

Approximately 40 million people go on camping trips in the United States each year. Not surprisingly, the number among those who pitch a tent and forgo the pleasure and convenience of indoor plumbing is considerably fewer than that. Camping out today increasingly means trailers, campers, vans, pop-ups, and, to a lesser extent, truck-mounted caps and slide-ins.

According to online sales reports, RV shipments in the United States were right around 500,000 units in both 2017 and 2018 (2017 was a record-setting year with 504,600 units). That's a whole lot of campers, trailers, and vans out on the roads—especially when you factor in all the vintage models out there. And although more RVs are manufactured in the US than in the rest of the world combined, it's really a worldwide phenomenon. (Amazing factoid: more than 80 percent of all RVs made in America are manufactured in just one state: Indiana!) It's been estimated that the RV industry has an economic impact of $50 billion in the US alone. The industry encompasses more than 22,000 businesses and provides nearly 300,000 jobs. It's a big business—really big.

According to a University of Michigan study commissioned by the RV Industry Association, US RV ownership has reached record levels. Believe it or not, about 10 million American households now own one. Multiply that times 3.2 people per household, and that's a whole lot of people hitting the road in campers. The typical RV owner, according to the same report, is married and has an above-average annual household income of $62,000. RV owners also are likely to own their homes and on average spend three to four weeks on the road annually. They're smart and generally pretty happy folks. Who wouldn't be, owning an RV?

Campers and trailers from the 1950s and 1960s are especially appealing with their bright colors and bright trim. These were often matched by bright colors and trim on the interiors as well.

Hudson Super 6 1929 towing home made caravan on U.S. 101 near King City, California 1936

In the early days of camp trailers, people handy with tools would often build their own trailer, like the plain-sided camper seen here. The tow vehicle, by the way, is a 1929 Hudson Super Six, a big car with plenty of power.

ON THE ROAD

So why do people go camping? According to a survey conducted by a large campground association, the three main reasons people say they go camping are to "reconnect with nature," "reduce stress and relax," and "spend more time with family and friends." However, it's interesting to note that one of the amenities people care most about when selecting a campground is free Wi-Fi access! Maybe that's one reason for the popularity of campers. People may love to get away from it all, but they also like to take a significant part of "it all" with them. And to do that, you have to have room, such as you get in a camper, trailer, or van. And if that camper, trailer, or van happens to be a vintage unit, so much the better.

Old campers are loaded with retro chic, a certain old-fashioned charm that's just not available in a modern unit, even the so-called retro-styled ones. As in art, nothing beats an original. Picture an old Winnebago with walnut wood inside and maybe shag carpeting or funky linoleum floors—cool stuff. Or imagine an old Airstream trailer with jalousie windows and aluminum walls. Perhaps a romantic weekend in a tiny Scotty camper for two?

Kabin Koach trailer built in 1936

This 1936 Kabin Koach trailer has handsome "streamline" styling inspired by the modern airplanes of that era. The roof vents kept things cool inside, as did the small windows.

Naturally interior space varies quite a bit on trailers according to their width and length. When buying, try to find one that appeals to your sense of style and history, and one that is also big enough for your usage.

No, these ladies are not "Sisters on the Fly." They appear to be winners of various beauty contests. Terry was a long-lived camper brand, beginning in 1948 and ceasing production in 2009.

Women on the Move...

With a focus on the great outdoors, ultrapopular travel club Sisters on the Fly has members in all fifty states and Canada, Australia, and France. In addition their Facebook page has more than 150,000 followers. Their motto? "No men, no kids, be nice & have fun!" Sounds like an idea that a lot of ladies could get behind.

Until the problem of fitting a serviceable toilet inside a camper was solved, some enthusiasts came up with unique "solutions."

The First Modern Camper

No one could ever hope to pinpoint when the very first camp trailer was built—except that someone has attempted to do just that. A whole bunch of people actually.

One of these claims pinpoints the first camper to 1904, built by a horseless carriage company and designed to be pulled by a Model T Ford. That would be a great story, except the Model T didn't come out until 1908. Others point to the 1910 Pierce-Arrow Touring Landau, a sort of camper car that debuted at Madison Square Garden in 1910. The Landau was a beautiful automobile with a fold-down rear roof so passengers could enjoy fresh air while touring. It was factory-equipped with a backseat that folded into a bed, a chamber pot toilet, and a sink that folded down from the back of the driver's seat. The driver—usually a professional chauffeur—was connected to his passengers via telephone! This was a handy vehicle to have in the days when "motor hotels" (a.k.a. motels) were practically unknown and hotels were often of uneven quality.

Also built in 1910 were camp trailers made by Los Angeles Trailer Works and Auto-Kamp Trailers. Although production wasn't large, the campers caught the public's fancy wherever they were seen. Over time dozens of manufacturers began producing what were then called auto campers.

Some point to the 1910 Pierce-Arrow Touring Landau, a sort of camper car that debuted at Madison Square Garden in 1910, as the first camper.

On top of it all, there are so many places to take vintage campers, even if you confine yourself to traveling just in the US. The United States alone has fifty-nine parks operated by the National Park Service, an agency of the Department of the Interior. The National Parks are protected areas established by acts of the United States Congress. Some are larger than our smaller states. The first national park, Yellowstone, was signed into law by President Ulysses S. Grant in 1872, followed by Michigan's Mackinac National Park in 1875 (decommissioned in 1895), and Sequoia and Yosemite national parks in 1890. The Organic Act of 1916 created the National Park Service "to conserve the scenery and the natural and historic objects and wildlife therein, and to provide for the enjoyment of the same in such manner and by such means as will leave them unimpaired for the enjoyment of future generations." Amen to that! Throw in hundreds more National Forests, state parks, regional park systems, privately run campgrounds, and Canadian provincial parks, and your options are inexhaustible.

Too small a trailer can make things tight when company comes over for lunch. For situations like this, it makes sense to bring along a pop-up shelter for entertaining outdoors.

Besides, when you have a vintage camper, anywhere you can legally park it is your campsite—and it doesn't have to be in the woods. It might be the back parking lot of Home Depot, your mother-in-law's side yard, or a pretty patch of woods next to a bubbling brook three towns over. It's all good. But first here's an explanation of the various types of camping available.

Tramping, Camping, or Glamping . . .

Tramping . . . in which you sling onto your back a pack containing food, supplies, bedding, and a tent. You wear a canteen on your belt, along with a knife, rope, compass, and emergency medical supplies. Think of hiking on the Appalachian Trail during a rainstorm or marching through the outer reaches of Zion National Park in midwinter. You get to pee in the woods, swat flies and mosquitos to your heart's content, and sleep on the ground along with the ants, bugs, and maybe snakes. If that sounds a little too much like being on bivouac in the army, you're right.

Camping . . . in the context of bringing a wheeled shelter with you, is a much more civilized activity. You attach your pop-up camper, camp trailer, or fifth wheel to your car or truck and load it up with everything you think you need: food, supplies, a boat on the roof, bicycles or scooters tied on back, laptop, and beer. Plenty of beer. You don't want to be getting thirsty when you're out in the woods many miles from the nearest package store.

Or you can load up your converted van, bus, or slide-in camper and hit the road for fun and adventure. Some of the nice things about all this are no hotel bills, no restaurant bills, and you're probably saving on your utility bills as well, since you're not at home using electricity. And you get to stay where you want to stay. In your own camper bed!

Or, if you want, you can rent a vintage camper at one of dozens of campsites that offer the vintage camper experience at a daily rate. These campgrounds usually feature completely restored campers of various makes and models, grouped together in a pretty spot.

Camping actually became a big fad in the 1920s and 1930s when famous people like Henry Ford, Thomas Edison, John Burroughs, Harvey Firestone, Glenn Curtiss, and others made headlines in the newspapers and newsreels of the day while "tenting out" (or caravanning, as it was sometimes called). It became a fashionable thing to do and newspaper reporters wrote reams of stories about the adventures of Mr. Ford and his friends as they traveled and camped. There were already a good number of companies building and selling travel trailers. Most of those early businesses are long gone, but a few survived to this day. More about that later.

Glamping. Looking for luxury and a unique experience? Maybe you should try glamping, a portmanteau for "glamorous camping."

Camping with Sherlock Holmes

Sherlock Holmes and Dr. Watson decide to go on a camping trip. After a hearty dinner and a bottle of wine, they lie down for the night and go to sleep. Several hours later, Holmes awakes and nudges his faithful friend:

"Watson, look up at the sky and tell me what you see."
  Watson replied, "I see millions of stars."
  "And what does that tell you, Watson?"
  Watson pondered for a minute. "Astronomically it tells me that there are millions of galaxies and potentially billions of planets. Astrologically I observe that Saturn is in Leo. Horologically I deduce that the time is approximately a quarter past three. Theologically I can see that God is all powerful and that we are small and insignificant. Meteorologically I suspect that we will have a beautiful day tomorrow. And what does it tell you, Holmes?"
  Holmes was silent for a minute, then spoke: "Watson, old chap, you've entirely missed the point. Someone has stolen our tent!"

Here's another big streamliner, though it's difficult to make out what brand it is. Judging by the cars, it appears to be circa 1936. The location is Bay City, Michigan.

By 1976, Serro Travel Trailers had expanded well beyond its adorable little Scotty and was building larger trailers with more room and more amenities. The brand name is now owned by another company that claims to be preparing to offer Serro trailers once again.

With glamping you can rent a vintage camper or trailer, or even a vintage motorhome, that's been fully restored and upgraded to the height of style and luxury. (Glamping also includes exotic tenting locales, yurts, and cabins, which are outside the scope of this book.) Picture a vintage Airstream trailer on the roof of a hotel in London, or a pack of vintage trailers set up in a remote and beautiful location out West, with luxury accommodations and fantastic side trips to box canyons and remote mesas included. Add in champagne delivered daily and chocolates on your pillow every evening and you're getting the idea. That's glamping, man.

The popular website Glamping Hub (www.glampinghub.com) lists thousands of available properties, although most are some sort of cabin, treehouse, yurt, or lodge. However they do have more than 200 listings for camper and van rentals, and these are mostly vintage-type campers and trailers, as well as camper vans. They offer all sizes of trailers imaginable, as well as exotic and secluded destinations that guarantee a lot of fun. Some sample choices: a cool vintage "canned ham" trailer in Oracle, Arizona, or maybe you'd prefer a hippie-style converted van in San Francisco (where else?), or perhaps a vintage Airstream near White Sands, New Mexico, or, for the really adventurous, a fully restored VW Camper in Cornwall, England. Or how about a cozy vintage Shasta trailer in Maine? There's even a double-decker bus for rent that has been fully converted to camper duty.

Colorful postcards were especially popular with campers as an inexpensive way to keep in touch with the folks back home.

One idea for finding the trailer of your dreams is simply to go to a campground and if you see a camper you like, ask if it's for sale. A better idea is to look on Craigslist, as well as some recommended vintage camper websites.

EASING INTO THE HOBBY

Renting a camper is a good way to check out the ins and outs of the hobby before you buy. One popular website for renting vintage campers is Vintage Camper Share (www.vintagecampershare.com). This site offers "vintage RV rentals delivered and equipped with supplies for easy-peasy fun!" Their website is great to visit for the vintage camper pictures alone, and it's a great resource for getting into vintage camping.

Other vintage resources include The Camper Concierge (www.thecamperconcierge.com) in the Dallas/Fort Worth area, Little Vintage Trailer (www.littlevintagetrailer.com), and the appropriately named Great American Country (www.greatamericancountry.com). You can also check out Pinterest, which has a great deal of information on vintage camping.

A typical family camper site in the 1960s. All the usual neighborhood dynamics occurred in these communities, just on a seasonal basis.

WHERE TO BUY ONE

Now that you're interested in vintage campers and trailers, the big question is where do you find one? Believe it or not, one of the best places to look is in your own town. You can usually locate a decent used trailer somewhere nearby, a fixer-upper you can restore if you're handy with tools. It's likely you can find a really nice old Airstream, Argosy, or Winnebago, and more, if not all, sitting forlornly in backyards and fields in your hometown, or within an easy drive of where you live. With a little cleanup (okay, maybe a *lot* of cleanup) and mechanical repair, they can be made ready for the road. Repack the wheel bearings and put on new tires, to be on the safe side, and you're good to go.

Not finding what you want around town? One of the best online sources for vintage campers/trailers is the classified advertising section of www.vintagecampertrailers.com. You can expand your search by looking on Craigslist or, better yet, place a wanted ad on Craigslist or other social media sites stating you're in the market for a nice old camper. You'll be surprised at what turns up. Another option is *Hemmings Motor News'* online or print editions under "RVs for Sale." But first read this book in its entirety before you go shopping or

The Early Camping Pioneers

The group of famous men, the so-called Vagabonds, probably did more than anyone to popularize the idea of camping in the early days. The group consisted of some of the most famous men of the era: Thomas Edison, Henry Ford, Harvey Firestone, and naturalist John Burroughs. From 1913 to 1924, they traveled about the country in automobiles during their annual camping trips. Although at first they were able to do so with a degree of privacy, in time the trips became widely covered by the media, which published numerous magazine and newspaper articles about them and even featured them in the weekly movie newsreels that were shown in movie theaters. All this publicity—these men were heroes of the age—evoked a desire in others to go car camping, although, truth be told, most regular folks didn't have the means that Henry Ford had. The Vagabonds, after all, brought with them a custom Lincoln truck outfitted as a camp kitchen and staffed by a chef. While they actually slept in tents, their widely chronicled adventures helped promote car camping and the RV lifestyle.

Years after the Vagabonds were gone, CBS News correspondent Charles Kuralt captured the romance of life on the road with reports that started in 1967 and wore out a series of motorhomes while covering more than 1 million miles over the twenty-five years of his immensely popular television program, On the Road. *Kuralt* became a folk hero among Americans yearning to see more of the country.

searching. You want to become as well-informed as possible before you slap down your hard-earned dollars on a vintage camper.

If you're interested in buying a vintage camper, the time to get in is now. The hobby is growing by leaps and bounds and prices for vintage campers and trailers have shot up in the past years. They will probably continue to increase as more and more people become acquainted with the hobby. Collecting and restoring an old trailer or camper can be fun as well as lucrative when you go to sell your project. Good hunting!

Ultracool: a 1957 Oldsmobile hardtop sedan alongside a color-matched trailer of unknown make, although after careful research of old trailer designs, our best guess would be that it's a Kenskill.

Beginning in the 1930s, larger trailers required larger automobiles to pull them. The 1946 De Soto being used by a modern-day enthusiast to tow their vintage canned ham is probably a bit of overkill. The setup sure looks cool though!

By the mid-1930s, trailers were becoming more streamlined and stylish. These two 1936 Airstream Silver Cloud models provide a good example of changing tastes in trailer style and design.

A mid-1920s camper trailer and automobile. Note the large crank-out windows and nice curtains. Smaller, quality-built trailers like these were a boon to young families looking for adventure.

Early camper trailers weren't exactly lightweight. Presumably the V-12 under the hood of this Lincoln Zephyr was sufficient to get this young family and their trailer to a favorite fishing hole.

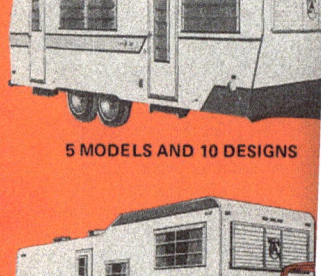

In 1970, Wheel Camper Corporation of Centreville, Michigan, offered a fairly wide range of towables, from small pop-ups to big fifth-wheelers. Their pop-up featured an airlift roof system to eliminate the need to crank to open up the trailer.

Even the more modern styling of this 1978 Terry trailer is appealing nowadays because it's so reminiscent of the '70s. Fluted side paneling and a colorful strip add a nice touch of style to the unit.

The 1950s brought us the canned ham look as exemplified by this cute little Shasta, a circa 1959 model. Note the jalousie windows and the small propane tank, that indicates this unit has a stove inside.

Should this circa 1961 Shasta be considered a tin can or a canned ham? Truthfully it has styling elements of both, but overall it leans more toward the canned ham look. And this ham has wings!—a Shasta design touch for several years.

CHAPTER TWO

Tin Cans, Canned Hams, Wooden Teardrops, and Camper Trailers

Do you love traveling to remote places and seeing things that most other people never get to see? Do you think the idea of parking a vintage steel-shelled trailer under a star-filled sky in the middle of the Western desert sounds appealing? Like the idea of sharing a cozy double bed with the one you love in a place far from the crowds and noise? Do you think the sound of raindrops pitter-pattering on a tin roof are romantic? Don't mind using a toilet in a bathroom that's smaller than a telephone booth (do you even remember those?)? Then you just might have what it takes to be a "tin-can tourist."

TIN-CAN TOURISTS

Generically speaking a tin-can tourist is anyone who loves camping in a vintage camper or trailer, especially one that's made of metal. But to be completely accurate, the term originally came about as a slang reference to the canned food that early trailer tourists usually brought along on their trips. Their provisions had to be canned because the early camp trailers didn't have proper refrigeration—heck, a lot of them didn't even have electric lights, so folks brought along a lot of canned goods and purchased perishables like milk, eggs, and other fresh essentials along the way, ensuring a nice mix of foodstuffs, fresh and canned.

Nowadays a lot of people refer to any collector of vintage campers as a tin-can tourist. In this usage the tin-can part of the name, of course, refers to the material used to build many (though not all) of them. (Although metal, it's not usually tin but instead a light-coated steel or aluminum). Most vintage trailers from 1950 on are metal-clad, while the earliest ones were made of wood.

But to be a true card-carrying "Tin-Can Tourist" (capitalized, no less!) you have to claim membership in a very special club for enthusiasts called the Tin-Can Tourists (www.tincantourists.com). This organization's members have been enjoying the great outdoors for more than 100 years. The Tin-Can Tourists were originally founded during 1919 in Desoto Park in Tampa, Florida. About a year later they received their official state charter. The club said its objective was "to unite fraternally all autocampers," which is what folks who owned campers and trailers were known as at the time.

Yes, They Did Have Principles
The guiding principles of the original Tin-Can Tourists, and the basic precepts they hoped to promote, were

> *Clean camps*
> *Friendliness among campers*
> *Decent behavior*
> *Plenty of clean, wholesome entertainment for those in camp*

Thanks to the growing popularity of camping, the new group expanded rapidly during the 1920s and '30s. Members inducted fellow campers through an initiation process that included teaching the prospective member the group's secret handshake, sign, and password. Then, after singing the organization's official song, "The More We Get Together," *voila!* The camperite was an official member of the Tin-Can Tourists of the World.

The club grew rapidly, but by the mid-1920s, Tampa residents were getting sick of their park being taken over by the campers, whose vehicles tended to chew up the landscaping. To discourage the campers, they began shutting down the park a month early in

Another canned ham is this 1950 Fleetwood trailer being towed by a good-looking Dodge convertible that appears to also be of 1950 vintage, perhaps a Canadian model.

With smooth, rounded shapes, the 1930s-era trailers were meant to be streamlined for easier towing. Units like this usually have a double bed, small kitchen area, and a dinette.

One of the earliest metal trailers was the aluminum-bodied Bowlus Road Chief. Quite advanced for its time, the design (as well as its tooling) was sold at auction after the company went bankrupt. The Bowlus concept eventually became the basis for the very successful aluminum Airstream trailer.

March. Undeterred the Tin-Can Tourists moved their winter get-together to nearby Arcadia, Florida, which welcomed them with open arms—as well as a specially built campground.

What happened after that is an interesting story: Although in the early days some towns shunned the Tin-Can Tourists, when the Great Depression hit in late 1929, various Florida communities began to compete for the privilege of having the Tin-Can Tourists set up camp in their towns. The townspeople realized that having thousands of campers coming to town to purchase food and other supplies would provide a huge boost to the local economy. During the Great Depression, that was no small accomplishment.

Although the Tin-Can Tourists thrived as an organization for decades, by the 1980s it had almost faded away, a victim of neglect. Even then, however, a few diehards still got together on occasion to share a meal and talk of old times.

Then, in 1998, enthusiasts Forrest and Jeri Bone decided to revive the club as an "all make and all model" vintage trailer and motor coach club. They held a renewal gathering at Camp Dearborn in Milford, Michigan. For its first event as a newly revived club, some twenty-one campers and trailers attended what was called the May Renewal Gathering. By the end of that year, fifty lucky people were accepted as charter members of the renewed version of the Tin-Can Tourists. Since that time, the group has continued to grow and holds regular gatherings in Michigan and Florida, as well as regional rallies at a slew of locations across the United States. In addition regional representatives have been added for England, Japan, and France. This new rendition of the Tin-Can Tourists is open to all tin can–hauling campers and its goal is to abide by the original group's objectives and guiding principles, as well as the promotion and preservation of vintage trailers and motor coaches and the exchange of information and experiences.

One of the best features of the Tin-Can Tourist website is that it includes advertisements for used vintage trailers and campers, a big help if you're in the market for one.

An Old Camper Saying

The Good Lord made shinbones strictly to help people find their trailer hitch in the dark!

Canned Hams: A Different Type of Tin Can
Maybe you're more of the "canned-ham" type of vintage tourer. A "canned ham" is a vintage camper trailer that looks a lot like one of those inexpensive canned hams you see in the grocery store—you know, kind of oblong and slab-sided. You're probably wondering exactly what the difference is between a tin-can camper and a canned-ham camper. Well, you might say it's a matter of degrees. Any canned ham is, by its very nature, a tin can. But not every tin can is a canned ham, because a lot of tin cans don't look like a canned ham standing on its side. Some are rounded, some are square, some are round with square corners, and a few tin-can trailers are even two stories tall! Another way of looking at it is that "tin can" refers to the material the camper is made of, while "canned ham" refers to the overall shape of the unit. So, generally speaking, if it's metal, it's a tin can (or maybe a canned ham), but if it looks like it should be wearing a colorful label from Hormel or Swift, it's definitely a canned ham.

A very interesting website dedicated to canned-ham travel trailers is www.cannedhamtrailers.com. It's chockful of information, restoration tips, stories from owners, and other resources.

Some notable brands of canned hams include the ever-popular Serro Scotty, which is a small but pretty camper with the classic shape and bright color schemes that recall the canned ham's glory days of the 1950s and 1960s. Scottys are the preferred camper for folks who need a lightweight trailer because they lack a truck or large car to tow a larger trailer. The Scottys don't take up much room in the driveway, either, and they have well-arranged interiors that usually include everything you need for comfy camping—all while retaining that classic look everyone loves. A bonus: due to their popularity, a lot of them are still around, so prices tend to be very reasonable. Another popular brand of canned ham is the Shasta which, like Serro Scotty, is still being made today.

It's up to you to decide how involved you want to get in restoring a vintage camper trailer. Some units you'll find just need a good cleaning and a little paint and perhaps some new appliances. Others, well . . .

Canned-ham trailers are among the most popular collectible vintage trailers, with their whimsical appearance and easy towing. The downside is they tend to be on the smaller side and can feel cramped if used for long trips. But for weekend getaways, there's no better fun.

Here's a lovely 1957 Comet camper trailer with an equally lovely 1957 Chevy. Canned hams can still be found at reasonable prices and are fun to restore.

The ever-popular Serro Scotty trailers are fairly easy to find at reasonable prices. They don't take up much room and are sturdy, so owners don't junk them unless they're completely shot. Restoration is fairly simple too. This family sure seems to love theirs!

So How Do You Stay Fresh in the Can?

Although most new campers have built-in showers, and some even have outdoor showers, a lot of the earliest vintage campers and trailers don't. The question becomes how do you stay fresh in the can? There are a few options. One is to haul in a bucket of water and give yourself a sponge bath. Another is to go for a swim every day. But a better choice is to choose campgrounds that offer shower facilities (most do). Those facilities are also larger than the phone booth–size ones in many campers. Many campgrounds also offer recreational activities for adults and kids alike.

The badge on the side of this tin-can trailer appears to say "Goodnight"—a brand we're not familiar with. However, that's not unusual; there are literally hundreds of defunct trailer brands and thus far no one has compiled a complete record.

Boles-Aero made a lightweight aluminum-bodied ham in the 1940s and 1950s. They're a little rare today but quite collectible. According to www.tincantourists.com, Boles-Aero trailers are "a high-quality aluminum trailer amongst the best built and most beautifully finished trailers ever produced . . . [and] have always been highly regarded for their rugged aircraft riveted construction and utilitarian beauty. . . Many believe the 'Canned Ham' era (1946 to 1959) Boles Trailers are the most beautiful, with the gleaming aluminum exterior."

Other vintage canned-ham brands include Avalon, Aristocrat, Comet, Terry Rambler, Gypsy, Kenskill, Corvette, Jubilee, Price, Crown, Hanson, Forester, Cardinal, Dalton, Siesta, Little Caesar, Fan, Mercury, Little Gem, Aladdin, Yellowstone, Lakewood, Deville Vagabond, and literally dozens more. In the 1960s, Winnebago, better known for its larger campers, even produced a series of smaller canned hams that make for very nice collectibles today.

Canned hams are among the most collectible of vintage trailers and campers, mostly because they look so cool. The retro shape and especially the retro interior trim many of them have make them the sort of trailers that will always be in style. They definitely stand out in a crowded camper park. Be prepared for lots of visitors anxious to get a better look inside your vintage camper. And it seems the older the trailers are, the larger the crowds they attract.

Are you now thoroughly confused with these vintage trailer types? If so, please don't cry any wooden teardrops. Those are next!

A cartoon postcard circa 1949.

While this photograph came to us with no notation, judging by the shape of the windows and body shell, we're fairly certain it's an Airfloat, probably of late 1930s vintage.

This circa 1935 Airstream is a classic teardrop trailer. Although this predates the aluminum Airstream models, even here Airstream's commitment to streamlining is evident, with the gently curved roof and front-end structure, plus the gracefully streamlined teardrop rear.

Wooden Teardrops

The wooden teardrop style of vintage trailer usually dates to the earliest beginnings of the travel trailer hobby in the 1920s and 1930s. That also explains why they look the way they do: in the art déco period, the look of aerodynamic streamlining was all the rage. Rounding off the forward face of a trailer and sloping the roofline back to the tail, creating a teardrop shape, was considered the last word in streamlining. Designers felt that streamlining gave the trailer a look of the future: sleek, efficient, and ultramodern. An added benefit was reduced air drag at speed, which meant the car's motor didn't have to work so hard and the driver could maintain a higher speed and climb mountains more easily.

The interior of the Airstream teardrop is snug but cozy, with a small dinette, sink, and counter space. Notice how everything inside is made of dark wood, handsome in appearance but lending to a dark interior.

Teardrops tend to be on the small side, a result of the era in which they were first produced. Cars of the 1920s and '30s were lightweight and often featured small engines with not a lot of excess horsepower and torque. The Ford Model A, America's favorite car for a time, offered just 40 horsepower; even a comparatively big car like a 1932 Nash Ambassador produced only 125 horsepower.

Teardrops are almost always built of wood, usually a hardwood frame covered in something light and inexpensive like plywood. This helps keep weight down and also makes them relatively easy to assemble—and fairly easy to restore today.

As far as brands go, there were hundreds of companies making teardrops back in the day. In its earliest days, Airstream produced very pretty teardrops made of wood, which are highly prized today. Airstream switched to aluminum-covered teardrops just prior to its switch to the classic Airstreams we all know and love.

One favorite teardrop camper is the plain but lovely 1940s-era Alcoa, which has a polished aluminum skin like an Airstream, but with a classic teardrop shape. Other classic brands include Benroy and Kamp Master.

During the filming of the 1936 movie Banjo on My Knee, *actress Barbara Stanwyck was supplied with this teardrop trailer to use as a portable dressing room and for resting between takes.*

Believe it or not, the five trailers seen here circling a small garden area are all Airstream models, including the first of its aluminum luxury trailers.

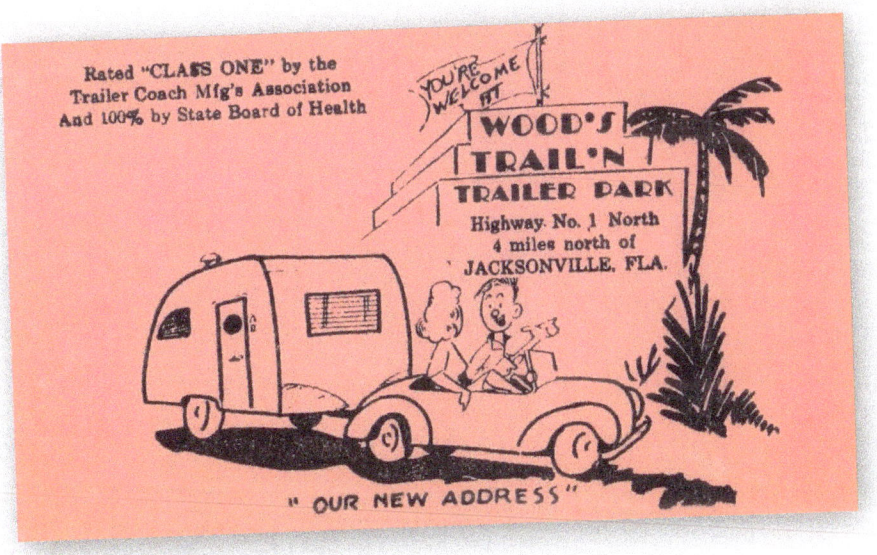

Even in the early days of camping, it behooved campgrounds to stress the safety and cleanliness of their facilities.

Although they tend to be on the petite side, the teardrops usually have a small double bed for two people, generally in the rear of the trailer, along with a chair or two to sit in, a sink, and perhaps a small gas stove, plus a small area for food preparation. What they don't usually have is a lavatory. So the idea is to stay at campgrounds with facilities or, if you're farther afield, bring along a bucket with a lid and a small shovel for burying your waste. If that sounds smelly and distasteful, it is. It's also a big reason why many folks avoided camping in the early days. In fact it was the wife of an engineer/camper enthusiast who finally pointed out the problem, prompting him to come up with the flush toilet, sink, and shower seen in modern campers today.

Wooden teardrops are by far the coolest and most vintage of all vintage trailers but because of their age they have certain limitations and drawbacks. They tend to be smaller than later models, they tend to have fewer luxuries (if having a toilet can be called a luxury), and it's much harder for the restorer to find authentic original parts. On the plus side, they are also usually much lighter than newer trailers, meaning they're easier for a vintage car to tow and, being made mostly of wood, they are easy to repair, assuming you're handy with wood. And of course, in doing a restoration one can always upgrade the cabinets to a fancier wood or add even some extra storage space. Who besides you will know it's not original?

A larger circa 1937 Airstream teardrop trailer is seen in downtown Tombstone, Arizona.

Judging by the coupe alongside it, this is a late 1930s trailer, a canned ham with no label, to use a pun.

Although large camper trailers were seen in the 1930s and 1940s, the relative prosperity of American families in the 1950s led to larger-size trailers becoming much more common.

VINTAGE CAMPER TRAILERS: THE BIG BOYS

For people who have to have the most room possible, the choice is simple: get a camper trailer. These are the big boys of the vintage camping hobby, the roomiest and the heaviest, riding the longest chassis and able to haul the family and all its "essential" stuff. Among the most popular brands to look for are Westwood, Roadmaster, Airstream, Vagabond, the biggest of the Shasta and Kenskill models, Aladdin, and Winnebago.

In addition to more room and comfort, the bigger camper trailers boast more convenience features like built-in radios, awnings, and the ever-important bathroom. Another nice feature is that, being mostly self-contained, they can be pressed into service as an extra guest room while parked at home.

The bigger trailers allowed for more room inside and interiors became much more civilized, as seen in this 1953 model, which looks like the living room of a small New York apartment!

Whether it's a tin can or a canned ham, a vintage trailer is fun to take on vacation.

WANT TO CHEAT A LITTLE BIT?

Okay, let's say you've been unable to locate a good restored vintage trailer and you lack the skills to restore one yourself. Or let's say you're too lazy to be bothered with either but you want to join the vintage camper movement and love the looks of old campers. Good news for you, my somnolent friends: there are plenty of new retro-look trailers and campers available. One company, Riverside RV in La Grange, Indiana, produces a line of campers that replicate the looks of the classic 1960s campers, with two-tone paint schemes, and interiors with wood cabinets and Formica countertops. The look is authentic 1960s, but the amenities are up to date, including wet bath (some units even come with a full bath), conventional and microwave ovens, sound systems, and more. Some models even offer a slide-out compartment for additional living space.

Of course, you always have the option of buying a nice used camper of more recent age but with that vintage look. A few short years ago, longtime camper manufacturer Shasta produced a replica of its classic 1961 model, right down to the two-tone paint. Although no longer in production, used models come up for sale occasionally and make a dandy camper with vintage looks and modern conveniences. The same is true of CH Camper, a company no longer in business. They produced a very attractive replica of a circa 1950s small canned-ham trailer. If you can find a good used one, grab it!

Stretching things a bit, there's the Happier Camper company (www.happiercamper.com) that makes a little ham roll of a camper that isn't a replica of anything that comes to mind, but certainly looks retro, with bulging rear fenders and a rounded, egg-shaped body that is too cute for words. Tiny and just 1,100 pounds (499kg), the thing can be towed easily by just about any kind of a car and manages to provide room for eating, sleeping, and what have you in an incredibly efficient package.

WHAT IS A FIFTH-WHEEL, ANYHOW?

A small part of the collectible trailer market is dedicated to owning and restoring vintage fifth-wheel trailers. What are they? They're travel trailers that tend to be larger than average and can be towed only by large pickup trucks that have a special platform (called a fifth wheel) installed in the truck bed. The trailer itself has a mating surface with a pintle-style hook that fits into a slot or hole in said fifth wheel, similar to the setup used by tractor trailers. Fifth-wheel trailers are a relatively new development, so you're unlikely to find one older than 1960s vintage.

Setting Up Camp

A loaded minicamper pulled into the last remaining campsite. Four children instantly leaped from the vehicle and began feverishly unloading gear and setting up the campsite. It was like watching a well-rehearsed dance number. Kids rushed to gather firewood and help their mother set up the camp stove, dinner table, and cooking utensils. They helped to unfurl the awning and set up a pop-up shelter tent nearby. One camper who watched all of this happening said to the children's father, "Congratulations that's a really impressive display of teamwork. How do you get them to cooperate so well?" The father replied, "I have a very simple system: no one gets to go to the bathroom until the camp is set up."

A fifth-wheel trailer is the type that is not towed via a bumper hitch, but instead has a pintle that inserts into a circular lock (i.e. fifth wheel) in the bed of a pickup truck, like this 1996 Integrity. For the record, in the late 1920s and into the 1930s, some fifth-wheel trailers hooked into a lock in the trunk of a tow car.

As trailer travel transitioned to recreation in the early twentieth century, some of the early pioneers in the camper-trailer game got ideas from Conestoga "covered wagons" of old. In fact one early leader in the industry, Covered Wagon Company, took their name from those bygone conveyances.

CHAPTER THREE

From Covered Wagons to... Covered Wagons

Let's face it: America is a land of travelers and movers, a nation of nervous, antsy people who are always ready to pull up stakes and head somewhere else (anywhere else!) at the drop of a hat, sometimes in search of a better opportunity or a better home, and just as often simply for the hell of it. Over the years, the country has had several especially big migrations, including the legendary Mormon Trek in the nineteenth century, the great influx of poor Irish after the Potato Famine in the mid-1800s, and the vast migration of black Americans who moved north searching for work and a more welcoming land during the mid-twentieth century.

Probably the largest American migration, however, was the one that began in the period during and just after the Civil War, when millions of Americans, some longtime residents but many of them newly arrived from Europe, packed up their covered wagons and headed west where there was still plenty of room and land was cheap, oftentimes given free by a government that wanted to see America grow. Huge wagon trains slowly traversed from Ohio and Missouri to the western half of the country, some traveling as far as Washington state. For black slaves recently released from bondage, the idea of traveling far away from their former lives seemed worthwhile, though it must have been enormously frightening. Despite the special hardships they had to bear, thousands of former slaves chose to join the great westward movement. It's how the West was settled.

The covered wagons that these diverse folks traveled in were often the legendary Conestoga wagons which, though not the first camper vehicles, can be considered among the very earliest campers in America. They carried furniture, bags of seed, farm equipment and tools, food, water, medical supplies, and anything else the travelers could squeeze in, along with tents for camping in along the route. But many migrants chose to sleep inside the wagons at night, preferring the comfort of an enclosed structure to the questionable pleasures of sleeping outside on the ground. They would help unload the wagons, then pull out a comfy featherbed and blankets and sleep in solid indoor comfort. Just like being in a modern camper.

AMERICA'S REAL FIRST CAMPER VEHICLES

For thousands of years before European settlement, some of the North American continent's original settlers, American Indians, traveled about, following the seasons and food sources. Some of these cultures utilized what later came to be called *travois*, which, if we use our imaginations, can be considered forerunners to campers. A *travois* is a platform or netting mounted on two long poles lashed together in the shape of an elongated triangle. The narrower part of this frame is pulled by a horse or person, while the two broadly spaced ends are dragged along behind. The netting between the poles is piled with food, clothing, supplies, and weapons.

The American Indians of the Plains tribes often used travois to move from campsite to campsite. Much like a modern camper, the triangular devices held their sleeping arrangement as well as food supplies. America has a long history of people on the move.

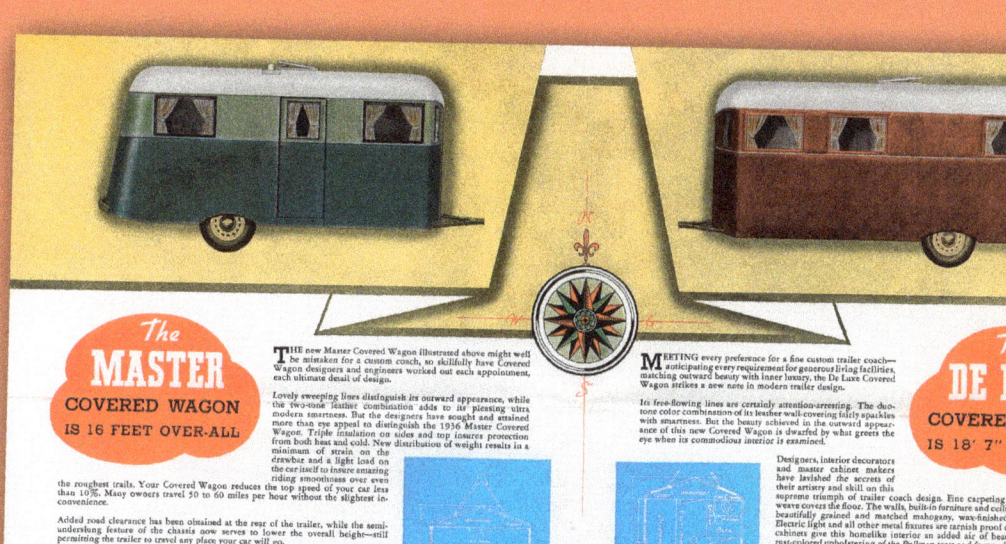

*The most popular camper trailer brand of the
1930s and early 1940s was the famed Covered Wagon.*

Flash forward to America in the early 1920s. Some of the early pioneers producing later-day camper-trailers got their idea for these vehicles from the Conestoga wagons of old. Wally Byam, the founder of luxury trailer maker Airstream, created his first camper simply by installing a tent on a flat platform built atop an old Model T chassis. From such small seeds grew a new industry.

A SLOW START

The camper industry got off to a fairly slow start. In 1930 there were only forty-eight trailer manufacturers in the United States, mostly small, regional builders that lacked countrywide sale networks. In addition recreational camping in an enclosed vehicle was still a relatively new phenomenon. It takes time for people to get used to a new idea and camping out in a trailer was definitely a new idea. However beginning in the early 1930s, interest in campers and sales of trailers took off. Strangely the Great Depression, the huge catastrophic economic collapse that began at the end of 1929, proved a boon to trailer makers as thousands of Americans took to the road in search of opportunity or just a job. By 1937 the recreational camper industry had grown to more than four hundred builders in the United States alone.

The Covered Wagon Company
The industry leader by far was a manufacturer called, appropriately enough, the Covered Wagon Company, which produced more than 10,000 trailers a year, making it a thriving million-dollar business in a decade when thousands of old-line, long-time manufacturing companies, and tens of thousands of small businesses of all types, were going belly-up. Wall Street was in a panic, stock prices were in freefall, and stockbrokers were jumping out of skyscrapers.
 Covered Wagon was successful for many reasons. The exterior design of the Covered Wagon camp trailer featured styling that people loved. The body was rectangular with rounded corners, sort of like a big loaf of bread. In that regard it was similar to other trailers on the market, but the Covered Wagon's unique roofline made all the difference. No matter what color you chose for the body, the roof was painted a contrasting color, usually white, with downward-heading peaks that imitated the look of the covered wagons of the Old West. In fact the earliest Covered Wagon models featured an actual canvas top. The trailers usually were fitted with generously large windows, giving them a feeling of roominess and light inside, as well as very nice interior fittings. And unlike most of the other firms, which used cheap plywood and Masonite to construct their trailers, Covered Wagon boasted a steel-covered body with sturdy wood framing.

The Covered Wagon name was well known in America and when they announced new models— as in this 1936 sales brochure—it was big news in camper circles.

The Covered Wagon Company was founded in Detroit in 1929 by Arthur Sherman, who had inherited Sherman Laboratories from his biologist father. Sherman came up with an idea for a new and improved camper after a rather unsatisfactory experience with a tent trailer during a family camping trip. He felt that, even lacking experience, he could design a better camper for his family than the one they'd just endured. He soon came up with one boasting the iconic styling that his children dubbed "covered wagons" after the legendary prairie wagons of old.

Believing there was potentially a fair-sized market for his design, Sherman rented a garage, hired a couple of cabinetmakers, and began building travel trailers. When he showed off his trailer at the Detroit Automobile Show in January 1930, it received a very enthusiastic reception. The next year, the fledgling concern sold a reported 117 trailers. His company grew year by year. In 1934 a total of 340 Covered Wagons were produced. Sherman decided to take a gamble on mass-producing trailers, figuring that the market was ripe and that by producing trailers in large volume he'd be able to offer a good product at a bargain price.

His gamble paid off handsomely. In December 1935 scores of Covered Wagons began to roll off Sherman's brand-new assembly line in Mount Clemens, Michigan. The production plant was located at 332 Cass Avenue in the former Copeland Products factory, where refrigerators had previously been built. Incredibly by the spring of 1936, trailer production was running at the level of almost 1,000 units per month, a previously unheard-of volume, and additional factory space was needed to keep up with soaring demand. Sherman leased production space at two other locations in town. In time the company became Mount Clemens' leading employer, with over 500 workers on the payroll. It also became the leading manufacturer of camp trailers nationwide as well. Incredibly all of this had gotten its start despite the economic hardships of the Great Depression. In fact sales of Covered Wagons set records throughout the 1930s.

The Covered Wagon Company was responsible for several innovations in the trailer industry, including the use of electric trailer brakes as standard equipment, which proved to be a major safety improvement. The firm also developed an exclusive and patented exterior covering that it called Shermanite, which was formed by combining zinc-coated steel and plywood to create a sturdy, weatherproof exterior skin that looked nice and was durable and easy to clean.

The Covered Wagon name was well known in America and when they announced new models—as in this 1936 sales brochure—it was big news in camper circles.

The Covered Wagon Company was founded in Detroit in 1929 by Arthur Sherman, who had inherited Sherman Laboratories from his biologist father. Sherman came up with an idea for a new and improved camper after a rather unsatisfactory experience with a tent trailer during a family camping trip. He felt that, even lacking experience, he could design a better camper for his family than the one they'd just endured. He soon came up with one boasting the iconic styling that his children dubbed "covered wagons" after the legendary prairie wagons of old.

Believing there was potentially a fair-sized market for his design, Sherman rented a garage, hired a couple of cabinetmakers, and began building travel trailers. When he showed off his trailer at the Detroit Automobile Show in January 1930, it received a very enthusiastic reception. The next year, the fledgling concern sold a reported 117 trailers. His company grew year by year. In 1934 a total of 340 Covered Wagons were produced. Sherman decided to take a gamble on mass-producing trailers, figuring that the market was ripe and that by producing trailers in large volume he'd be able to offer a good product at a bargain price.

His gamble paid off handsomely. In December 1935 scores of Covered Wagons began to roll off Sherman's brand-new assembly line in Mount Clemens, Michigan. The production plant was located at 332 Cass Avenue in the former Copeland Products factory, where refrigerators had previously been built. Incredibly by the spring of 1936, trailer production was running at the level of almost 1,000 units per month, a previously unheard-of volume, and additional factory space was needed to keep up with soaring demand. Sherman leased production space at two other locations in town. In time the company became Mount Clemens' leading employer, with over 500 workers on the payroll. It also became the leading manufacturer of camp trailers nationwide as well. Incredibly all of this had gotten its start despite the economic hardships of the Great Depression. In fact sales of Covered Wagons set records throughout the 1930s.

The Covered Wagon Company was responsible for several innovations in the trailer industry, including the use of electric trailer brakes as standard equipment, which proved to be a major safety improvement. The firm also developed an exclusive and patented exterior covering that it called Shermanite, which was formed by combining zinc-coated steel and plywood to create a sturdy, weatherproof exterior skin that looked nice and was durable and easy to clean.

Free! HERE'S YOUR NEW VACATION HOME!
25 COMPLETE TRAILER OUTFITS made up of
25 "COVERED WAGON" TRAILER HOMES and 25 NEW 1937 FORD V-8 SEDANS
AND 1000 GALLONS of SINCLAIR H-C GASOLINE FREE WITH EACH OUTFIT

Highlights of the NEW 1937 FORD V-8
Model offered is new Tudor Sedan
Power—V-8, 85 horsepower, Ford engine gives quick acceleration and power. **Easy-Action Brakes**—Ford brakes give you "the safety of steel from pedal to wheel." **All-Steel Safety Body**—Top, sides and floor welded into a single unit of great strength. Safety glass standard all around. **Riding Comfort**—A big, roomy car with extra space in the body. Exceptionally large luggage space.

Highlights of the "COVERED WAGON" Trailer Home
Model offered is new, 1937, De Luxe Model, 19-foot Trailer Home
Brakes—Electric, standard. **Chassis**—All-steel electrically welded. Great tensile strength. **Coupler**—Permits full turning in any direction. **Windows**—Eight double-strength steel sash and frames. Cannot break apart. **Interior**—Furnishings include beds for four, wardrobe, cupboards, ice box, floor covering, stove, kitchen sink, screens, lavatory, lights. Special construction for strength and insulation.

EACH TRAILER OUTFIT COMPLETE AND READY TO TRAVEL. Completely equipped for four people with: Silverware (Tudor plate by Oneida Community Silversmiths); Cannon towels, bed linen; Cannon blankets; Federal cooking utensils; Revere copper skillets; china; electric bulbs—and a plentiful supply of CAMAY!

With the Great Depression over, it was time for American companies to begin promoting their products. In this 1937 ad, Camay Soap had a contest to win one of twenty-five new Covered Wagon camper trailers, each one fully equipped right down to the silverware, along with a new Ford V-8 sedan to tow it with!

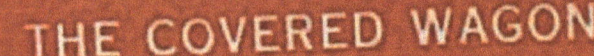

This circa 1939 postcard describes the big new Pacemaker trailer by Covered Wagon. Notice the price—just $298! For comparison, the car—a 1938 or so Nash—would have been around $850.

Over the years, the Covered Wagon company offered many different models, from budget-priced standard models to extra-fancy deluxe models, and they ranged in price from a mere $395 to over $1,200, depending upon the options that the customer selected. Eventually things on the assembly line grew too complicated, so the product offerings were pared down to just three models to facilitate more efficient production. Those products were illustrated in the company's 1937 color catalog as the Master, Deluxe, and Custom models.

The market for travel trailers remained a dynamic, growing field and over the next few years dozens of additional new competitors appeared. Unfortunately more than a few of them were shady outfits that built substandard units. Working in cramped quarters with day laborers slapping together plywood and Masonite to produce cheap, easy-to-sell travel trailers without regard to quality or durability, the products of these fly-by-night outfits hurt the image of the entire industry while stealing sales from established firms that built quality products. Other new companies lacked adequate financial reserves and found themselves in bankruptcy, leaving thousands of customers high and dry with new trailers but no access to spare parts or warranty repairs.

But that wasn't the case with Covered Wagon. The company remained the largest trailer manufacturer by far, with a big factory, a handsome and well-planned product line, and the ability to purchase modern tooling for excellent quality and mass production. But as big as Covered Wagon was, there was room for innovative newcomers like Airstream, whose unique and modern design helped the nascent company thrive.

Naturally the above history begs the question, where is Covered Wagon today? It's an unfortunate story. World War II affected the company greatly, as it did many American manufacturers, sometimes being beneficial, othertimes causing a company's downfall.

Dusty Old Joke

Q: Why don't mummies go camping?
A: It's so relaxing they're afraid they might unwind.

Once America entered the war, Covered Wagon converted its production plant to build military products for the war effort, just as thousands of other American companies did. Utilizing its construction skills, the firm produced truck cargo bodies for the military and proved so efficient that it was given the Army-Navy "E" award in the spring of 1945 for high achievement in war production.

However, following the Allied victory in Europe, the War Department drastically decreased its orders for truck bodies, which of course hurt Covered Wagon. Lacking war work, and with needed materials in short supply and nearly no market for vacation campers at the time, the company found its production lines completely idle by mid-1945. With virtually no income, in September of that year, Covered Wagon management decided to lease the firm's main production plant to the Ironrite Ironer Company, which began producing its Ironrite household clothing ironers there. At the time, Covered Wagon officials expressed their intention to resume trailer production "after reevaluating the company's position," but for some unknown reason production never resumed and the famed Covered Wagon Company passed into the pages of history. It's a shame, because they really were a superb trailer maker, and one can only hope that someday another firm will assume the old brand name and introduce a new Covered Wagon camper. (Today there is a trailer company in Georgia called Covered Wagon, but they make cargo trailers, car haulers, and concession trailers, not campers.) The former Covered Wagon factory in Mount Clemens was razed in July and August of 2013.

Here we see temporary housing during World War II in the form of Covered Wagon campers. The situation looks quite domestic, with small fenced-in yards and family names on signs. There also appear to be utility poles bringing in electricity and phone service.

This old press photo has no identification, but it appears to be the early 1940s. Notice the neighborhood location and the wooden sidewalks— this appears to be wartime housing for the men and women who worked in the defense factories.

By the mid-1960s, slide-in campers were becoming very popular—they offered a lot of amenities at a reasonable price (a lot less than a towable camper)—and they could go deeper into the woods, especially if carried by a four-wheel-drive truck like this 1967 Jeep Gladiator.

CHAPTER FOUR

Pickup Shells and Slide-in Campers

History books tell us that the first light-duty pickup trucks produced in the United States debuted during 1918 and were built by Chevrolet. However, light-duty pickup trucks didn't really take off until seven years later, when Henry Ford introduced a factory-built pickup in 1925 on his bestselling Model T chassis. Ford was the largest automobile company in the world by a huge margin, so when they introduced a new product, people took notice. It also helped that the new Ford was the lowest-priced truck on the market with a base price of just $281. That bargain price tag included a 20-horsepower four-cylinder engine, a two-speed planetary transmission, a stylish open roadster body with a folding soft top, and an all-steel bed with four stake pockets and an adjustable tailgate. Not surprisingly Ford sold more than 33,000 of the lightweight trucks in the first year of production, a huge success by the standards of the day. Even company managers were surprised by the popularity of the new light commercial vehicle. Other companies soon joined the pickup fray—Willys-Overland, Dodge, International Harvester, Studebaker, and REO, to name a few. By the time World War II broke out, the US light-truck market was strong and growing.

TRUCK-MOUNTED CAMPERS

There are two basic types of truck-mounted campers: camper shells and slide-in campers. The camper shell is usually (but not always) a hard fiberglass unit that mounts atop a pickup bed and encloses the cargo area. It sits atop the box sides, usually rising 1 to 4 feet (0.3 to 1.2 m) above the top edge of the box. When designed for camping, these units generally include opening side windows and a rear door with either a fixed or opening window. Headroom is quite limited; camper shells are definitely made mostly for sleeping. Sure you can sit up and read a book, but overall, camper shells are not very comfortable as living quarters. Still they're certainly more comfortable than sleeping on the ground and offer much better protection from the elements than tents.

Slide-in campers are much larger units that also sit atop the pickup bed. Rather than mounting atop the box, however, they slide into the bed and boast a tall roof that allows their owners to stand up inside. They also usually include kitchen facilities and room for a family to sleep inside (oftentimes including a loft that projects over the pickup cab. Some vintage slide-in units even include rudimentary bathroom facilities as do most modern units.

Every camper's worst dream—taking off and leaving someone behind—is well illustrated in this comic postcard that dates from the early 1960s.

Another really excellent combination would be this 1963 Studebaker Champ pickup truck carrying a sweet little 1963 Highway Cruiser pickup cap.

This photo doesn't identify the make of the slide-in camper, but the truck is a 1960 GMC—and this would make a really nice combination to own today. Part of the fun of vintage slide-in campers is finding a vintage truck to carry it.

One of the earlier slide-in campers was the Sloat; a 1959 model is shown here. Sloat bragged that its camper came with standard equipment that included a clothes closet, linen closet, two large kitchen cabinets, a breakfast nook that converted into a double bed, and a sleeping compartment over the cab. Their motto? "Apartments for Pickups."

Given the history of light trucks in America, it's somewhat surprising that camper shells didn't really come into their own until the 1950s. Sure it probably wasn't very long after that first Model T appeared that someone installed some sort of sleeping arrangement in the bed, but truthfully, light trucks back then were small and usually too cramped for use as a camper. If anyone tried to install a camper shell on a truck, it would have been a homebuilt unit, and probably on a heavy-truck chassis. The Ford's four-banger just didn't have enough grunt to haul a heavy camper shell at a decent road speed.

However, as light trucks grew in size and power, by the late '50s, full-width truck beds provided a much wider base on which to install a camper shell. The gorgeous 1955 Chevrolet Cameo pickup and the 1957 International Harvester Golden Anniversary pickup, for example, were among the first to offer stylish "townside" bodies that eliminated bulging old-fashioned rear fenders in favor of a sleek look. Neither design added a tremendous amount of carrying space but did provide a wider base for mounting a camper. Floor space was significantly larger as well.

FIRST CAMPER SHELLS

The first light-truck-mounted camper shells debuted not long after the wide-side truck beds, though most initially were produced by camping-gear retailers. Often the campers were built from scratch in the back room of the retailer's store. One such outlet was Campway's in Santa Rosa, California (still in existence and found at www.campway.com). Early on the retailer hand-built slide-in campers, but as demand grew, it became obvious that hand-building slide-in campers and shells wasn't going to keep up with demand. Luckily several companies stepped into the void to begin production of factory-built shells.

Gemtop was probably the largest of the shell manufacturers. For decades they produced standard-sized camper shells and slide-in campers out of fiberglass. A wide network of dealers sold and installed their products. Gemtop shells were usually white in color (a sort of attempt to imitate the look of the old covered wagons) and featured sliding side windows for ventilation. They were produced to fit nearly every pickup available and in the 1970s were especially popular with the compact Japanese pickups that were all the rage at the time. The company's shells grew more stylish as time went on. Designers styled them to look more integrated with the trucks and gave them fancier window treatments as well as a broad range of color choices. In many cases they could even be ordered to match the truck color.

Other companies making shells included Brahma, Snugtop, Stockland, and Leer, the latter being particularly popular. Today Snugtop and Leer are still very popular brands and have been joined by a raft of newer companies. The new models are very comfortable, but nothing beats a vintage shell for cool.

Less popular, but still used today, are tent-style camper covers. With this type, a canvas or vinyl-coated cloth "tent" fits over the pickup bed, with movable brackets to raise the height of the cover when stopped for the night. These little pup tents are generally purchased to provide ease of setup and weather protection at a nominal cost. They usually provide enough interior room for occupants to sit up for meals and conversation but lack room for standing within. They may not be very comfy or warm, but they are cheap and easy to use: just adjust the top brackets to the open position for maximum room, throw in a couple of sleeping bags and a cooler with food and beverage and you're set. A battery-powered lantern is nice as well, and don't forget a radio or portable TV.

The chances of finding a vintage tent camper are pretty slim. Eventually the fabric wears out, tears, or simply rots from exposure to the sun and the rain. If you're lucky, you might be able to find one that's new old stock (NOS) and still in the box. Alternately you may be able to find an old tent camper frame and have a new fabric top made for it.

Slide-in campers made even more sense if you already owned a pickup truck like this stylish 1967 Dodge, on which is mounted a 1967 Camp Mate camper.

Camping Semantics

"Camping out" is sometimes defined as "the only vacation where you work harder cooking and cleaning and taking care of your living space than you do in your own house."

These canvas or treated cloth-type camper covers were never very popular because they tend to leak, and they offer little in the way of heat retention. But they were cheap to buy, and many rugged hunter-types purchased them as a step up from sleeping on the ground.

ENTER THE SLIDE-IN

Not long after the debut of camper shells, enthusiasts began to fit slide-in camper units to pickup trucks. Like the smaller shells, these began as hand-built units, at least until a few companies began offering factory-built slide-in campers.

Unlike the shells, though, slide-in campers existed as specially built units for a long time before a mass-production industry got in gear. They were almost always hand-built, one-of-a-kind DIY units with designs and quality that varied greatly, depending on the builder's imagination, skill, and materials.

Notice the stylish lines and interesting details on this 11-foot (3.3 m) truck camper by Franklin Coach Company of Nappanee, Indiana. Called the Franklin Silver Leaf, it features a three-burner range with oven, double sink with splash guard, plus a dinette that converted into a double bed. The truck is a 1968 Ford.

Camp Humor

In Alaska, tourists are warned to wear tiny bells on their clothing when hiking in bear country. The bells warn away most bears, but not all. Tourists are also cautioned to watch the trail for bear droppings to indicate the presence of grizzlies. One can tell grizzly bear scat from that of other bears because it has tiny bells in it.

This slide-in camper is not identified and we're not sure what brand it is. The side door helps to provide more usable space inside. The truck is a 1968 International Campermobile, all ready for camping adventures.

Logging Miles

One amazing example of the homebuilt type of slide-in trailer is the famous Nash Travel Log, crafted by the renowned outdoorsman and entertainer Charles Kellogg around 1917. Kellogg, known to audiences as "The Nature Singer" for his ability to imitate dozens of bird calls, found a fallen redwood tree and decided to build a camper out of a 22-foot (6.7 m)-long, 11-foot (3.4 m)-tall section of it. The log weighed fully 36 tons (33 metric tons)! To make the log into a house trailer, he slowly carved out the center by hand and then leeched out as much sap as possible. By these methods he was able to reduce the log's weight to eight tons—still a huge load.

There weren't many trucks that could carry that much weight back then, but the best of them was the famed Nash Quad, one of the earliest four-wheel-drives on the market. Built by the Nash Motors Company, it was an incredibly rugged vehicle, quite able to handle the weight of Kellogg's camper home, though its top speed was limited to less than 20 miles per hour (32kph). Amazingly, even with that severe speed restriction, Kellogg drove his camper across the US and back (twice!) in an effort to stir ordinary citizens to help save California's giant redwood trees. At the time, logging companies were petitioning the US government for the right to cut them down. Thankfully they were refused.

Starcraft was one of the most popular slide-in trailers during the 1960s and 1970s. The Jeep Gladiator four-wheel-drive trucks offered a special heavy-duty model designed for trailer carrying and could travel far off road where other trucks couldn't go. These are 1969 models.

A 1970 model El Dorado slide-in camper rests atop a sturdy Dodge truck in this advertisement. It's a W200 Camper Special equipped with heavy-duty suspension, cooling, and brakes, along with four-wheel-drive.

The two earliest of what can be considered modern factory-built truck campers date to the mid-1950s and they seem to have appeared almost at the same time. One was the Cree Truck Coach, built in Saline, Michigan, by Howard Cree. The other was the Sport King, built in Torrance, California, by Walter King's Sport King Company. King's slide-in was probably not only the first truck camper in the modern era, his company also built the first cab-over camper (i.e., a slide-in camper with a small sleeping area extending over the truck cab). Mr. King built his first truck camper in 1945, intending to produce just one for his own use, but in time he realized there was a market for the units and began producing them commercially. Sport King really popularized the idea of truck campers and, besides slide-in units, expanded into the production of Class C motorhomes, travel trailers, and fifth-wheel trailers. However the company fell on hard times during the recession of 1979 to 1985 and never quite recovered. Sport King ended production of recreational vehicles after the 1987 model year.

These truck campers aren't limited to vintage models. Several manufacturers continue to build them, a testament to their functionality and popularity.

Since the early 1950s Alaskan Camper has been building the only hard-sided, telescopic truck camper on the market. The idea is to give campers plenty of comfort along with a low profile for a safer, more comfortable driving experience and better gas mileage. The earliest Alaskan Campers used a manual hydraulic hand pump to raise the top, but now utilize a pushbutton electric pump.

The long-established Hallmark Campers offers a variety of slide-in campers, including bed-mounted and innovative flatbed-mounted units. Like the Alaskan, they have telescopic roofs, but in the Hallmark the telescopic part is canvas cloth rather than hard sided.

Livin Lite Recreational Vehicles offers a range of conventional slide-in campers as well as towable campers. The truck-mounted units are lightweight, sleek, and very stylish. They manage to fit a comfortable 60- by 80-inch (1.5 by 2 m) bed inside, too, along with seating, an oven, refrigerator, and a bathroom.

MAXIMIZING SLIDE-IN SPACE

The only problem with a shell or slide-in camper is that the interior floor space is pretty much limited by the floor space inside the pickup bed, which is already limited by those wheel wells that bulge up from the floor. As you can imagine, the available floor space is rather tight, and that means that spending too many days on the road can sometimes lead to cabin fever. Camper manufacturers have been able to increase total interior space over the years, first by adding a two-person sleeping compartment overhanging the truck cab, then by adding a few feet of space onto the camper aft of the pickup bed. In more recent years, modern slide-in campers have even offered side- or rear-mounted slide-out compartments to expand sleeping space and provide additional interior room. A few companies now offer campers designed for cab and chassis trucks, which offer the best floor space you're going to find in a slide-in camper. However the best solution for the vintage camper enthusiast is to buy a truck with the longest bed and find a good used camper that fits it. For additional room, consider bringing along a screened wall tent to use as a living room or extra bedroom.

Ever wonder how you get your slide-in trailer cap on and off your truck? Here's how. If you mount your vintage trailer on a vintage truck, you don't need to do this unless you like to take the unit off during the winter. Most people leave them on year round.

The GMC Sierra Grande puts camping on a solid foundation.

Want to enjoy your next camping adventure?

Then make sure you put yourself on top of something solid. A pickup truck that's built by people who specialize in building trucks.

A GMC pickup is built just like the big ones you see hauling freight from coast to coast. It has double walls in the cab and load box, with insulation in the roof for added quiet. Inside, you can specify full carpeting, big, foam-padded bucket seats, a fully automatic transmission, even air-conditioning.

But most of all, a GMC is dependable. And that's what you need when you're carrying a home in the loadbed. Plus, you have a choice of high performance power from our new Invader V-8 engine series, including a 307 V-8, a 350 V-8 and a 400 V-8.

Cut yourself loose and go follow the trail you've never been down before. Catch a sunset, or the early-morning sound of a fresh mountain stream.

But first, see a GMC truck dealer. He can make it all the more exciting.

The GMC Sierra Grande features a new series of Invader V-8 engines, including a 307 V-8, a 350 V-8, and a 400 V-8. All three are designed for power and performance. Pick any one and you will come up with a whole new brand of pickup excitement. Heavy-duty rear-leaf springs can be ordered to give you a solid foundation for your next adventure.

GMC the truck people from General Motors

The large trailer atop this sharp-looking 1969 GMC is not identified and, try as one might, it can't be found pictured in any of the guidebooks. It's another one with the helpful side entry door.

This is probably the smallest factory-built slide-in camper ever offered. If not, it's certainly the most unusual because it included two carrying wheels in the back to help steady the unit on the road. Jeep offered these through its dealers, and a few have survived and have been fully restored. This one is a 1969 model.

THEY WERE KIDDING, RIGHT?

The award for the craziest production slide-in camper has to go to Kaiser Jeep Corporation, which in 1969 introduced a slide-in designed to fit the smallest American vehicle on the market: the Jeep CJ-5. This, despite knowing that the most functional camper shells are designed for larger vehicles. With a short wheelbase, a narrow tread, and a tall body, the CJ-5 was already a fairly tippy vehicle. Adding a tall, heavy slide-in camper made matters only worse.

Thankfully the company told prospective buyers they had to order the optional 155-horsepower V-6 engine rather than trying the Jeep's anemic standard four cylinder. A 4.88 rear axle ratio meant it had decent acceleration, though it did limit the top speed (which was probably a good idea anyway).

Despite its drawbacks, potential and real, the Jeep camper was a pretty amazing little unit. It could sleep four, and even included a sink and toilet with running water! The trick to fitting all this stuff into a Jeep-mounted camper was to make the camper longer than the Jeep, with its own set of wheels off the rear that created a longer wheelbase. The whole setup came with extendable poles underneath the edges so that the camper could be set up as a standalone unit, allowing use of the Jeep for off-road adventures. These camper units are very rare today and highly sought by vintage Jeep enthusiasts.

In fact, there are dozens of collectible slide-in campers to choose from, depending in what era you like best. Some names to look for are Amerigo, Delray Imperial, Coachmen, Knight, Starflight, Goldstar, Travel Lite, Lance, Chinook, and Fleetwood. What's especially nice about vintage slide-in campers is that pricing is usually much lower than other types. Maintenance cost is also much lower because slide-ins have fewer systems that can go wrong. Be careful, however, if the purchase includes a pickup truck. Consider them as two separate issues and get the truck inspected by a competent mechanic, just as you should have the camper inspected by a competent trailer service person.

There are dozens of vintage slide-in brands to choose from. The unit used in this Dodge ad has a handsome wraparound window in the overcab section.

TWO- OR FOUR-WHEEL-DRIVE?

That brings us to something for the vintage slide-in camper or camper shell newcomer to consider: just what sort of truck to purchase. As mentioned earlier, if you want to enjoy more room inside your vintage camper, you'll need to buy a big truck. But should you buy a two-wheel-drive pickup truck, or does four-wheel-drive make more sense? It's an important question because four-wheel-drive means greater safety and flexibility: you can travel in snowy weather much easier with a four-wheel-drive truck, for example. But the truck itself will likely cost more than a two-wheeler and gas mileage will be worse. Think about how you're going to use your camper before you decide what sort of truck to install it on.

Four-wheel-drive is a nice option to have on your pickup, because it makes the truck safer in summer as well as winter. It also helps take you further off the beaten path, to that secret fishing spot or a mountaintop camp area. This 1973 Jeep Gladiator J4000 with a sturdy cap on the bed would make a good hunter's truck.

Resource for Truck Camper Enthusiasts

I've searched the country to find magazines devoted exclusively to truck camper enthusiasts and found one with a pretty good website. It's called Truck Camper Adventure (www.truckcamperadventure.com), and to quote their website it's "a free online magazine offering news, reviews, travel tips, and information of interest to the truck camper community. We cover all types of truck campers at Truck Camper Adventure. It doesn't matter if it's a slide-in or a chassis-mount, a hard-side or a pop-up, if it's a truck camper and it's carried on a truck, we cover it. Truck Camper Adventure caters to the off-road, overland expedition crowd. We promote the use of our public lands through exploration, outdoor recreation, and off-grid camping. As a result, you won't find any ridiculous RV park ratings or top 25 campground lists on Truck Camper Adventure. Instead what you'll find are write-ups and tips on breath-taking destinations and off-road trails that can be explored and enjoyed in your truck camper. 'Get away from the campground' is our motto. . . . Aside from supporting the truck camper community, this site has only one agenda—to promote the use and enjoyment of our public lands through the use of truck campers and other four-wheel drive vehicles like Jeeps."

If you want to buy the biggest camper you can find, you'll need a big truck to carry it; something like this 1974 Ford Super Camper Special with its long 140-inch wheelbase, heavy-duty frame and suspension, and big V-8 engine.

Vintage camping is popular throughout Europe, as witnessed by this classic Citroen station wagon towing an attractive bubble-shaped trailer of unknown make.

CHAPTER FIVE

Vintage European Camping and the VW Phenomenon

Vintage camping is a big hobby throughout Europe and the British Isles. Every weekend people by the thousands head for the country in their campers and trailers ("caravans") for a few days of fun or extended relaxation. As in the United States, the vintage camper and trailer hobby is growing there as well. Although the variety and brands of campers are numerous, one vehicle stands out in the vintage camper hobby: the legendary Volkswagen Bus. It's the original camper special and a champion of the old camper hobby. That holds true in the United States as well as in Europe.

The VW Bus is an amazing vehicle that's gone by many names: Camper, Van, Samba, Kombi, Transporter, Campmobile—and that's just for the camping versions. The regular VW passenger wagon that spawned these ingenious campers was sometimes called the station wagon or Microbus but was usually referred to by owners simply the VW Bus. Volkswagen itself dubbed it the Type 2.

The idea for the original Type 2 was first proposed in April 1947, and it was meant mainly to serve as a vehicle to haul car parts around the growing VW factory in Germany. It seems a Dutch VW importer had hand-built a Beetle-based van to haul automotive parts. The little truck with the air-cooled four-cylinder engine worked out much better than the larger, more conventional vehicles they'd previously used. This inspired VW's engineers and designers to create a commercial vehicle that would boast an extraordinary amount of interior space, despite being based on the prosaic Beetle's rather short 94.5-inch (2.4 m) wheelbase. To achieve the cargo capacity desired, the body design basically had to be a large, tall cube with rounded corners. In the end, it was essentially a 170-cubic-foot (4.8 cubic m) cargo box on wheels—yet it looked great! In time it became a classic.

The original prototype was dubbed the VW Type 29 and was designed to carry a maximum ¾-ton (680kg) load, which was fine, considering the vehicle's small four-cylinder engine displaced just 60 cubic inches (990cc), along with its power rating of a mere 30 horsepower. A six-volt electrical system was standard. Somewhere during the development, it was decided that if the vehicle proved as good a hauler as the engineers thought it was going to be, the company would offer a version to the public. After all, this was just after World War II and Germany and all the rest of Europe still faced years of rebuilding their shattered countries. A good, low-priced

Nothing beats the styling of the original Volkswagen Type 2, whether it's a bus or a camper like the one seen here. The simplicity of the body lines and the creativity of the classic V-front paint scheme are timeless.

One of the great treats about going to a vintage VW camper rally is the chance to see so many older Type 2s on display, many in their original colors, some done up as hippy vans.

Don't be fooled by trick paint jobs like the one seen here. This is not an early Type 2 but is a second-generation model. It's easily identified by the one-piece windshield and the rectangular air intakes on the front.

This early Type 2 is all set up for a good night's sleep on a sandy beach somewhere nice. The green paint and oak interior trim are a nice combination, while the yellow curtains make it feel very homey.

This red VW Camper is ready for the road, complete with a matching trailer to hold a wall tent perhaps, or extra food and camping supplies. Notice the little trailer even has matching VW hub caps.

cargo truck that was easy on gas was sure to find a market. The first VW vans and buses went on sale in Europe in 1949. Volkswagen of America claims that the bus was first officially imported to America in 1952, although it appears that many of them made their way here before that, probably brought in by people who'd seen them in Germany.

The vehicle was an immediate success in the United States. Initially just two versions were offered: the eight-passenger Standard and the fancier (well, for a VW, anyway) eight-passenger Deluxe. Both were considered station wagons, although it wasn't long before owners began taking out the rear seats and installing beds, tables, and chairs. As sales grew, commercial versions were also soon available. There was even a pickup truck version that became surprisingly popular. However, a dispute known as the U.S.–Germany "Chicken War" quickly put an end to this pickup, at least in the United States. The Chicken War resulted when West Germany put a heavy tariff on imports of very low-cost US-raised chickens in order to protect their domestic chicken farmers. In response the United States Congress placed a heavy tariff on imported pickup trucks. At the time, the only pickups being imported from Germany in any volume were those produced by Volkswagen. The new tariffs killed off the VW pickup virtually overnight. However VW's popular passenger buses and vans, untouched by the tariffs, remained popular.

Both in the US and Europe, people began to realize the vans were ideal for camping. Small firms began to offer interior equipment that made it easier to camp out of the station wagons and vans. Soon European up-fitter and coachbuilding companies, eager for work, were turning out vans that were factory-equipped as campers.

In 1951 Volkswagen decided to cash in on what was now the trend of camping out in their retrofitted Kombi vans. The company introduced the Westfalia, so-named because it was retrofitted with camping equipment by Westfalia-Werke, a subcontractor in the Westphalia region of Germany. As built by Westfalia-Werke, the new VW camper van was fitted with real birchwood interior panels, laminated plywood cabinetry, an icebox, sink, water storage tank with pump, electrical hookups, screened jalousie windows with curtains, and a laminated folding dining table. Optional equipment included attached popup tops with canvas and screen sides, awnings and side tents, portable chemical toilet, camp stove, child's sleeping cot in the cab, large storage box matching the interior panels, rear swing table, and a small map table mounted on dash. The VW Westfalia camper proved surprisingly popular, particularly in light of Europe's still-struggling economy (recalling the camper's early success in Depression-era America).

Westfalia wasn't the only firm converting VW buses. In Kent, England, Martin-Walter produced the Dormobile, which featured a large cutout "door" in the roof panel that folded up and out to allow standing room inside the van and provide space for an upper berth for a child to sleep in.

VW Van Spotter's Guide

Few things are cooler than a VW Van. Although they were considered utilitarian back in the day, today they are considered works of art. The first series can be easily identified by their split windshield. These were produced from 1949 to 1967 and are by far the most collectible today. They were available in several configurations:

The VW Panel Van *is like the station wagon version except it has no side windows, just plain sheet metal, and also a vertical partition wall behind the front seats to separate the cab area from the cargo area—important in case of an accident or panic stop that might cause packages to fly forward toward the driver. The Panel Van was designed as a commercial model for transporting cargo. The cab area was finished with simple gray Masonite-style panels rather than the fancier cloth or vinyl seen in other versions. The cargo area was usually plain painted metal.*

The **Kombi**, *also known as the eleven-window bus, was the entry-level passenger bus. Its name denoted that this was a "Kombination" vehicle that could carry passengers (with the rear seats in place) or cargo (with*

The second-generation VW camper is, while not as collectible as the first series, quite nice to own and drive to vintage camper rallies. They are also less expensive to purchase, all things being equal.

Note the front-mounted spare tire on this second-series Type 2 camper. Hanging the spare on the front saves a lot of interior space while also making it easier to get to when needed. Some people like the look; some don't.

the rear seats removed). The Kombi was a simple vehicle outfitted very similarly to the Panel Van, with an interior covered in Masonite-type panels. Most factory-approved camper conversions (Westfalia, Sundial, Riviera, etc.) were based on the Kombi model, so this is the one you're most likely to come across if you're searching for a factory-built VW camper.

The **Microbus** and **Deluxe Microbus** nine-passenger (eleven-window) buses were essentially a VW Kombi with nicer interior trim (cloth or vinyl rather than hard Masonite), along with very stylish two-tone exterior paint choices. Like the Kombi, the rear seats could be removed, but the Microbus was mainly intended to carry passengers rather than cargo. The nine-passenger Microbus has bench-style seats throughout. There were also seven-passenger versions. In either case, the seats can be removed for camping purposes.

Doesn't this look like great fun? Camping out on the beach in your classic Type 2 camper. You live free and easy; the VW gets good gas mileage and you don't have to pay for hotel rooms!

Another United Kingdom conversion was the Devon Motor Carriage, a venture by JP White of Lisburne Garage. Boasting real oak cabinets, a two-burner stove, and a table/bench combo that converted into a double bed, the Devon (and Eurovette, another Devon camper product) was considered the finest quality and are highly coveted today.

A somewhat similar vehicle was produced in the United States in Washington State by a company called Automotive Service Incorporated (ASI), which offered a lovely camper called the Riviera. The VW-based Riviera boasted a large roof section cutout that rose up on scissor struts to provide a more uniform outside appearance and a maximum amount of extra headroom.

First series VW buses and campers can be identified by their clean, smooth styling with trademark bright trim moldings forming a large V on the front panel and flowing along the sides, along with the prominent circular VW badge set in the front V. Two-tone paint and gorgeous glass-covered headlamps are other style marks of these classic buses. A two-piece split windshield is featured, along with rounded turn signal lamps offset above the headlamps, and a curved front bumper painted white.

As far as collectability, the first series buses are the absolute tops, though the chance of finding a decent one for not much money is pretty slim. Prices range from under $10,000 for something needing a lot of work, up to $200,000 for an absolutely perfect bus. Shocked? Well, the average price for a nice example seems to range somewhere between a more moderate $40,000 to $70,000, with the price depending mainly on condition and features (though the 23-window versions are by far the most valued). As with the purchase of any old vehicle, you're better off buying the very best example you can

Just about any color looks good on a VW Type 2 camper but, to these eyes at least, it seems the brighter the better. VW offered really nice orange and yellow hues.

You'll notice the European license plates on many of the VW campers seen in this book, because many of the photos were taken in Europe where they are plentiful.

Time Machines or VW Buses

Believe it or not, the second series, or T2, of VW's Type 2 Bus remained in production in Brazil through the end of 2013. Wouldn't you like to go there right now and bring home a good, clean used one?

afford, as restoration usually costs quite a bit more than purchasing a vehicle that's already been restored. Exercise caution when buying and hire a competent mechanic who's familiar with VW buses to do a thorough inspection prior to purchase. If the seller is honest, he or she won't object, and it could save you a lot of heartache not to mention money. Have your VW expert examine the vehicle for rust and rot as well as mechanical condition. Don't be surprised if repairs have been made in the past. These are old vehicles, after all. Also make sure to have any repairs checked for accuracy and quality. This will affect value too. A vehicle that's been properly restored to original condition is worth much more than one that's been repaired to other-than-original condition.

The second series of VW buses arrived in 1967 and are identified by their one-piece windshields and tighter, more "modern" styling. Rather than a large circled VW emblem up front they usually have a smaller one, along with two fresh-air intakes for the heating/ventilating system flanked by orange turn signal lamps. The bumper is short and can be painted or chrome plated. There are many

Amazingly, the Type 2 is only a little more than 1 foot (30 cm) longer than a VW Beetle, making them easy to park and maneuver in traffic. How they fit all that space in such a small area is a mystery.

Determining the Year of Your VW Bus

Beginning in October 1958, a vehicle identification known as the M-code plate was placed behind the right-hand front seat. This plate indicates the exact date of manufacture of your VW bus, along with which factory options it was equipped with, its export destination, its model number and layout, and important paint and upholstery color information.

On vehicles built prior to October 1958 there was no such plate, but a body number was stamped behind the front seat. Although the body numbers are sequential, they don't provide the same information as the later M-code plates. However, there is still hope for the collector determined to find out more about their classic VW: to obtain the most accurate information on your early Bus, you need to request it from the Stiftung AutoMuseum in Wolfsburg, Germany. Once you provide your vehicle identification number at the museum website, they can locate all the information on the car and (for a price) print out an official "VW Birth Certificate." This certificate (or zertifikat, as the Germans spell it) contains detailed information on the engine and transmission assembly (including dates), original exterior color, and interior and optional equipment. There's simply no better source of information about the original factory condition of your Volkswagen. Having a certificate will help in the proper restoration of your VW Bus, which is vital to enhancing its ultimate value. Having a birth certificate even allows you to celebrate your vehicle's birthday on the exact date it was produced.

Here's a factory advertisement for the 1977 VW Campmobile (US model). This year the VW's engine was upgraded with fuel injection for easy starts, more power, and better fuel economy—up to 28 mpg over the road.

improvements in the second series. The engine was upgraded to 1600cc pumping out a more credible 57 horsepower. The side air intakes were replaced by oval gills set in the upper corners of the rear. By 1972 the engine size had been further increased to 1700cc and dual carbs became standard, raising output to 66 horsepower. Thankfully front disc brakes became standard in 1971.

Other changes took time. It wasn't until 1974 that the Bus's old-fashioned generator was replaced by a modern alternator (most other auto companies had made the switch in the mid-1960s). In an effort to gain more power and improve drivability, fuel injection was introduced for 1975. The second series buses were produced until July 1979, after which they were displaced by the new VW Vanagon.

With its rear-mounted engine and rear-wheel drive, the VW camper offered better traction than most vans or wagons and thus could do a limited amount of off-road driving; important for getting to campsites that include hidden streams and beautiful fields.

95

Vanagon
AND VANAGON CAMPER

The original Vanagon line—a 1982 model is shown here—was directly descended from the Type 2 but offered modern styling, more convenience, and greatly expanded powertrain options. These are beginning to attract attention from collectors.

The Vanagon's interior offers plenty of room as well as the necessary appliances and counter space. You may want to check these out, as prices are very reasonable at the moment.

Although not nearly as valuable as a collectible, at least at the moment anyway, the VW Vanagon is a very interesting vehicle. The early models were still powered by a classic air-cooled VW engine, but could be ordered with either a four- or five-speed manual transmission or a three-speed automatic. As mentioned, styling is more modern than the prior generation, being sharp-edged and boxy, and because they look a lot like ordinary minivans, they don't attract nearly as much attention from bystanders. Later versions from the 1980s have water-cooled gas or diesel engines, and thus decent heating systems as well—a shortcoming in any air-cooled VW.

The Vanagon is a reasonable compromise for collectors looking for a bargain, because, although it's not as coveted as the early buses, it's much more pleasant to drive on long trips. It's not as susceptible to crosswinds, the heater works better, acceleration is quicker, and it can maintain a higher average speed, important on today's crazy highways.

How Slow Do They Go

All the old air-cooled Volkswagen models were famous for being slow, so VW decided to opt for a bit of self-deprecating humor. One memorable print advertisement offered the tongue-in-cheek headline "0–60 miles per hour? Yes."

The Vanagon eventually was replaced in 1990 by the Eurovan, a well-designed and very competent front-engine, front-wheel-drive van with a water-cooled engine. They're very nice but not cool—at least not yet. Give them a little more time to become collectible or take a chance that they'll grow in value and buy one now.

THE HISTORY OF CAMPING ACROSS EUROPE

In Europe, travel trailers and campers initially drew their inspiration from the Roma people who traveled from town to town in horse-drawn caravans, which is also how the term *caravan* came to describe what is known Stateside as a camper. Another big influence were the traveling showmen who spent most of their lives going town to town in horse-drawn vehicles equipped with sleeping accommodations. The famous British explorer Samuel White Baker actually bought a Roma caravan in Britain and had it shipped to Cyprus for his tour in 1879.

This European-spec Vanagon Westfalia is fitted with a high roof rather than a fold-up top. Notice the rolled-up awning on the side, perfect for providing shade for mealtimes and just hanging-around times.

The tiny camper towed by the equally tiny Austin looks like a caravan straight out of a Dickens tale. Vintage campers are a popular hobby in the United Kingdom and all of Europe.

The last iteration of the VW camper was the EuroVan, a 1992 model shown here. But VW is moving into trucks in a big way now, along with electric vehicles, and may introduce a new electric van. It's been hinted at.

This very attractive Viking camper, towed by what appears to be a modern SUV, was spotted at a vintage camper rally in the United Kingdom. Because of the smaller cars most Europeans drive, their campers tend to be on the smaller side, though this Viking is a nice size for any kind of trip.

Camping According to Charles Dickens

In England the origins of the caravan go back at least to the early 1800s. In Charles Dickens' novel The Old Curiosity Shop, published in 1840, Mrs. Jarley traveled the countryside with her waxworks show in a horse-drawn trailer that Dickens described as "not a shabby, dingy, dusty cart, but a smart little house upon wheels, with white dimity curtains festooning the windows and window-shutters of green, picked out with panels of a staring red."

The world's first trailer produced for leisure use is believed to have been built by the Bristol Wagon & Carriage Works in 1880 for Dr. William Gordon Stables, a popular author of teenage adventure fiction who specified that he desired a "gentleman's caravan." Eighteen feet (5.5 m) long and well equipped for comfortable travel, it was dubbed the *Wanderer*. Stables traveled the British countryside in it and later wrote a book documenting his travels called *The Gentleman Gypsy*.

By the turn of the century, caravanning was an increasingly popular activity in Great Britain and Europe. In 1901, the first dedicated caravanning club was established. The Camping and Caravanning Club (originally the Association of Cycle Campers) was founded by Thomas Hiram Holding, the father of modern camping in Europe. In 1907, the Caravan Club was founded with Stables as its vice president. Its stated aim was to "bring together those interested in van life as a pastime . . . to improve and supply suitable vans and other appliances . . . and to arrange camping grounds."

World War I and II interrupted the growth of the hobby in Europe. After World War II, many of the caravans produced were of the stationary type, meant to be cheap housing for people who had no homes and little money. They usually weren't very well built and, of

Europe has canned hams too, as proven by the tiny trailer seen here being towed by the equally tiny Austin Mini. Note all the trailers in this vintage photo; the Brits love their "caravanning."

course, couldn't be used for pleasure unless one had a unit installed in a vacation camp or near a body of water. But as the economy gradually improved, the lure of travel again took hold and Brits were soon back on the road to adventure.

During the 1960s, caravanning really took off in the United Kingdom. Improved manufacturing techniques reduced vehicle production costs, and makers were able to offer lower prices and higher quality. The units were now larger and more comfortable as well. Sleeping accommodations usually included a double bed and a bunk room, plus a dinette that could convert into a second double bed. The caravans also now had electric lighting. However it wasn't until the 1980s that a fully equipped caravan with hot and cold running water became the norm rather than the exception. The kitchens boasted full-size refrigerators and ovens. With hot showers and flush toilets, caravans finally became real homes away from home.

Only a small number of British camper-trailers have made it to the United States, usually imported by British ex-pats. Thus the chance of finding a vintage British camper in the States is rather slim. However if you do come across one, make sure to check it out—it could make for a very unique collectible vehicle.

What could be more fun than to be at the wheel of a gorgeous vintage Riley sportscar, towing an equally gorgeous vintage Winchester camper trailer? Note the righthand-mounted steering wheel and the vintage clothing the couple wears.

During a recent trip to France, I came across these campers near an old castle. Camping is alive and well in Europe, enjoyed by millions every week.

The brand of this handsome camper can't be made out, but the vehicle is a Land Rover Discovery. The photo was taken in France.

Resources for VW Camper Collectors

VW Camper owners, as well as those people in search of a vintage VW camper, will want to subscribe to VW Camper and Bus magazine. It's an extremely helpful magazine and readily available. As the website says, "VW Camper & Bus magazine is the number one worldwide magazine dedicated to the iconic VW Camper. It contains everything any Bus fan would ever need to know including news and products, entertaining and knowledgeable history features to a useful step-by-step How To section. The magazine also includes a variety of readers' content from inspirational road trips and stories to features on everyday Camper Vans."

Opposite: Regardless of what sort of camper you choose, vintage camping is all about being in the great outdoors and living life to the fullest. It's a great way to make family memories that last.

Above: This camper has a sideways-opening canopy, which is not often seen in the United States market. It provides more usable headroom than the slanted type.

Vacation time should be fun time, with equal helpings of activities and downtime. We all need to recharge our batteries from time to time; what better way than in a vintage camper trailer?

CHAPTER SIX

The Vintage Camper Life

If you really think about it, owning a vintage camper trailer isn't merely a matter of possession—it's an activity, a hobby. Depending on how hardcore you are, it could even be a way of life. Once you own a vintage trailer, you'll notice that your life changes in many ways. But to truly enjoy your new (old) camper you need to take it out on the road and really get involved in the hobby.

Joining a club is a good first step. There are several clubs to choose from. In addition to those mentioned earlier in this book—Tow Boyz, Tow Girlz, etc.—consider the following RV clubs too:

The **National Serro Scotty Organization** (www.nationalserroscotty.org) is a fun club that's also an extremely valuable resource for anyone owning or restoring a vintage Serro Scotty trailer. Their motto? "Cute Trailers, Friendly People and Awesome Adventures." Formed in 2004, it's a network of vintage Scotty owners and enthusiasts, boasting hundreds of members in every state except for Hawaii, plus Canada, Denmark, and Germany.

The **Family Motor Coach Association** (www.fmca.com) bills itself as the world's largest member-owned, nonprofit RV travel club. The FMCA claims more than 150,000 members and is headquartered in Cincinnati, Ohio. However, the club's target membership is owners of motor coaches (i.e., motorhomes), hence the club name. Although they claim to welcome trailer owners with open arms, you may feel out of sync showing up at one of their rallies with your vintage towable trailer. You won't look out of place if you're driving a truck-mounted camper shell, however, as these apparently are fairly common in the club.

Loving the vintage look of this circa 1951 postcard. It's an advertisement for a campground on U.S. 301 in Statesboro, GA. Today there is a campsite under a different name on U.S. 301, but it may be the same place just under new ownership.

Don't really care to camp out with others? It's easy enough to find a distant spot away from civilization for you to set up camp like this gentleman did with his Traveleze camper trailer and his 1959 Chevy pickup. Notice they're both painted the same color.

The Wally Byam Camper Club International and the Vintage Airstream Club (an interclub of the WBCCI) would both welcome the big Airstream seen out west in the 1970s. To qualify for membership in the Vintage Airstream Club, your trailer must be at least 25 years old.

Vintage Airstream Club (vintageairstreamclub.com) is an intraclub of the Wally Byam Camper Club International (WBCCI). The Vintage Airstream Club is dedicated to the preservation and enjoyment of classic vintage Airstream travel trailers, from the little single-axle Bambis to the longest Globetrotter. The Vintage Airstream Club website contains a whole history of the Airstream company, along with membership and contact info, a list of upcoming rallies and gatherings, club newsletters, and a slew of photos of vintage Airstream trailers.

The **Good Sam Club** (www.goodsam.com) bills itself as the nation's largest RV club, without the extra qualifiers of the FMCA mentioned earlier. Membership, their website says, brings discounts at the 2,400 Good Sam campgrounds nationally, along with help on trip planning, discounts on fuel and propane, and a lot more. Although the Good Sam Club is not a vintage camper club, per se, it's open to all types and years of campers and trailers and can be a good resource while on the road.

Camper owners and enthusiasts tend to be friendly, outgoing people. Many camping sites have organized activities for campers to enjoy, such as dances, entertainment, and cookouts.

The spartan accommodations of this family's prewar camper (possibly homebuilt) are a reminder of how far the camper advanced in just a few decades.

Jayco Travel Club (www.jaycorvclub.com) is another brand-related RV club focused mainly on modern units, though owners of vintage Jayco pop-ups and trailers will certainly feel welcome. With the stated aim of promoting family camping and gatherings of RV enthusiasts, the organization hosts one "international rally" each year in various locations around the United States and Canada. Other events include rallies in places from Nova Scotia to Las Vegas (there's even a yearly gathering at the Indy 500). If you own a vintage Jayco pop-up or trailer, this club is probably your best bet for finding vintage parts and service for your vehicle.

Any of these clubs can help you get more involved in the hobby. One really important service they offer is helping to connect you with like-minded enthusiasts and going on rallies, which means getting off your duff, piling your stuff into your camper, and taking it on the road.

VINTAGE CAMPER BRANDS: FIFTEEN FAVORITES

There are hundreds of vintage trailer and camper brands, not to mention pop-ups and slide-ins (mentioned in their respective chapters), but here are some of particular interest, beauty, and collectability:

Airfloat. Produced from 1930 to 1957, these stylish vehicles usually sported round windows and door openings like a cruise liner. Luxurious and commodious, they offered trailers up to a whopping 45 feet (13.7 m) long!

Above: This photo came to us undated, but judging by the clothing and hairstyles, we'll guess it's from the 1970s—a.k.a. the disco era. Note the vintage look of their trailer, with linoleum flooring, plaid seat cushions, and wood paneling everywhere.

Left: This 1961 Holiday House would make a real attention-getting collectible and has the bonus of being a really nice habit to spend some time in.

Aladdin. Built from 1963 to about 1973, Aladdin offered "a magic carpet to Vacationland." Mostly tin-can types, they've got interesting styling and rarity in their favor.

Bee-Line. With classic tin-can styling and bumblebee yellow-and-black paint schemes, these were smaller trailers aimed at weekenders.

Elcar. These were produced in Elkhart, Indiana, from 1936 clear into the late 1960s. Early models are easily mistaken for Covered Wagon brand trailers; later ones used more unique styling that's hard to categorize.

Fleetwood. Lasting more than fifty years in business, Fleetwood built canned hams and tin cans mainly in smaller sizes. Larger units were sold under the Prowler, Terry Coach, Wilderness, Taurus, and Avion brand names.

Go Tag-A-Long. A very popular brand from 1964 to 1988, building canned hams and tin cans with a unique trunk bump-out and turquoise-and-white paint scheme.

Haynes. After the Great Depression hit, automobile body-maker Haynes went into production with handsome trailers styled similar to the top-selling Covered Wagon. Extremely well built and highly desirable.

Kit. These trailers were teardrop-shaped and ran in size from 11 to nearly 20 feet (3.4 to 6 m) and always boasted good styling. Kit's first products were small teardrop trailers designed to hold camping equipment. You can still see them around vintage camper shows.

Little Gem. Little Gems are great because of their unique styling touches and good quality.

"M" System. With a classic breadbox styling, this brand offered commodious interiors and wonderful interior fittings that make these highly prized today. They were built from 1935 to 1960.

Camping out in a travel trailer means spending time relaxing with friends, having fun, and enjoying life.

Though unable read the brand name on this neat little canned-ham trailer, one can date the period by the car and the clothing—it's the mid-1960s, a great time to be alive.

Palace. With classic styling and up to three bedrooms, Palace trailers boasted breadbox styling and, after World War II, an aluminum frame and body.

Roadmaster. Looking for size and sweet styling? The Roadmaster, built from the 1930s to the 1950s, offered units from 20 to 35 feet (6 to 10.6 m), custom birch interiors, and a "skylite living room."

Spartan. There's nothing Spartan about the Spartan! These big (20 feet up to an amazing 45 feet (6 to 13.7 m) trailers were built by a company owned by J. Paul Getty. Introduced in 1945, they remained in production until 1961.

Terry. Like the Serro Scotty line, Terry trailers were designed to offer value for the dollar. With lengths of 12 to 19 feet (3.7 to 5.8 m), they are large enough for serious camping, yet light enough for a car or small SUV to handle.

Vagabond. Built from 1931 to the late 1960s, these are marvelous trailers. Prewar models have excellent breadbox styling while the postwar models have that "Fabulous '50s" look.

For some people, a quiet afternoon with a pipe, slippers, and a good book is a dream come true. Just look at the beautiful view he has—and the beautifully finished woodwork in this circa 1955 camper.

In the days before camper trailers had lavatories, even a primitive setup like the one pictured on this gag postcard would have been welcome.

THE NEXT STEP

So, what's the next step in getting involved in the hobby? How about going full immersion? Try going to a vintage camper rally. These events can be any gathering of like-minded individuals who happen to own campers and trailers. The Airstream Club and the Vintage Airstream Club schedule a rally every year and that attract scores of owners. They're big affairs, too, with live music, cooking exhibitions, entertainment and a whole lotta fun.

Some enthusiasts even like to dress in vintage clothing when they go on rallies, with fedoras and bowties for the men, bonnets and high-neck dresses for the ladies if you've got a 1930s-era trailer. Switch to porkpie hats and sheath dresses for the 1940s. Have a 1950s trailer? How about poodle skirts for the ladies, and snap jacks, rolled jeans, and slicked-back hair for the men? Naturally owning a vintage VW Bus means you've got to dress up in wild hair and tie-dyed clothing. For the right mood music, make sure to have "Alice's Restaurant" playing on the 8-track.

RECOMMENDED CAMPER READING

Depending on where in the hobby your interests lie, there are a number of books and magazines you might find useful and enjoyable. Some of the books may be out of print, but you should be able to find used copies through online searches. Here's a small sampling:

The Little Book of Camper Van. First published in the United Kingdom in 2007, this pocket-sized hardcover volume details the history of the VW Bus with a focus on the many camper versions

Camper on the Silver Screen

Clinton and Merle Twiss commissioned a 28-foot (8.5 m) land yacht for a road trip they wanted to take across America's then forty-eight states. The many misadventures that resulted on that trip inspired Clinton to write a humorous novel titled *The Long, Long Trailer*, published in 1951. The book subsequently was made into a comedy film starring Lucille Ball and Desi Arnaz in 1954, though an even longer 1953 Redman New Moon trailer was used in the film. If you're a Lucille Ball fan and haven't seen the movie, do so. It's a riot.

Vintage camper trailer owners should make a point of watching the Lucille Ball–Desi Arnaz screwball comedy The Long, Long Trailer, *which features a big 1953 Red Man New Moon trailer and lots of antics.*

While I endorse restoring a good, old camper, make sure to plan out a budget and stick to it. Don't buy the first old trailer you find; shop around and make sure you know what you're getting into. This sad relic is a good candidate for someone with a lot of restoration skill—and money.

offered over the years. Like the original, the latest edition is full of nice quality color and black-and-white photography and lots of information. It's something every VW Camper enthusiast should have.

Vintage Camper Trailers by Paul and Caroline Lacitinola is a hardcover book that examines the hobby by focusing on couples and individuals who own vintage campers. Written by two experts in the field, it's packed with terrific photographs of wonderful old campers and the fascinating people who own them. Put it on the bookshelf in your vintage camper. You're sure to love it.

Vintage Camper Trailer Rallies by Paul and Caroline Lacitinola is similar in format to their *Vintage Camper Trailers* book but focuses on the rally aspect of the vintage camper hobby. On vintage rallies, numbers of like-minded enthusiasts band together for a road trip. It might be a one-day event to a local campground or a days-, weeks-, or even months-long journey around the country. If you're planning on taking part in a rally, this is the book for you. The photographs alone are worth the price.

The Illustrated Field Guide to Vintage Trailers. Maybe you're looking for a certain style in a vintage trailer, or maybe you're looking at a neat old vintage trailer for sale but can't quite figure out what make it is. In either case this is the book for you. It lists hundreds of brands of vintage trailers, with illustrations of each and basic information on year, make, and even what models were offered. The color illustrations are a big help in determining what you might like style-wise in your next trailer.

Vintage Camper Trailers (www.vintagecampertrailers.com) is a bimonthly print magazine that "spotlights all aspects of the vintage camper trailering hobby." Inside you'll find pieces on preservation, restoration, and, of course, the fun to be had with them. A good resource for those already in the hobby and those who aspire to be.

Trailer Life magazine's (www.trailerlife.com) main focus is on modern trailers, but it can provide you with a quite a lot of basic information about camping and trailers in general, as well as various travel destinations you might want to try. After all, their staff are experts who have been camping for years.

Vintage Trailer magazine (www.vintagetrailermagazine.com) is also a good resource (www.vintagetrailermagazine.com). It is self-described as "the world's first magazine solely dedicated to vintage, classic, retro-styled, and custom trailers, vintage camper trailers, and travel trailers and those who love them." Also consider *Camping* magazine. It's not dedicated to vintage campers, or even just campers, but inside you'll find useful information on the outdoor life.

Heading out on the road in your vintage camper trailer means you can bring along your best friends with no hotel hassles. Cats and dogs and other pets easily adapt to life on the road—and they make it all the more enjoyable.

This American couple spent part of 1955 visiting Mexico in their roomy Airstream trailer. These are the kinds of memories you can make in a vintage trailer!

CHAPTER SEVEN

Silver Bullets: The Airstream Story

The king of vintage camper brands is Airstream. Yes a handful of makes are more beautiful than an old Airstream, and some are worth a lot more, but with those exceptions, it's fair to say that on the whole, vintage Airstream trailers hold their value the best, and are the most coveted brand in the hobby. Interestingly statistics show that on average Airstream trailers are on the road more weeks out of the year than any other trailer brand. That's because Airstream owners are travelers and adventurers. They yearn for the open road.

Airstream is also the oldest camper/trailer manufacturer in America. To understand Airstream better, you need to know a little of the history behind the product and the company that makes them. The entity that became known as Airstream was founded by a young man named Wally Byam in the 1930s. A magazine publisher and camping enthusiast, the story is that in the late 1920s, Byam had a wife named Marion who disliked sleeping on the ground in a tent. So he bought a used Ford Model T chassis—it was light and easy to tow—and built a sturdy wooden platform floor onto it on which each evening he would erect a tent when they stopped for the night. Although this setup was much more comfortable than sleeping on the ground, the tent was a pain in the neck to erect, and even then, Marion didn't care for it. A woman of culture, it was still much too primitive for her tastes.

In time Wally hit on the idea of building a teardrop-shaped wooden cabin on the Ford chassis, a primitive trailer home with just enough room for sleeping, as well as a small ice chest for keeping food fresh and a kerosene stove on which to cook. This appeased his wife—at least for a while.

When the stock market crashed in late 1929, leading to the Great Depression, tens of thousands of Americans lost their life savings. Some lost their homes and businesses as well, and many were plunged into crushing debt. One expense that was easy for consumers to cut was magazine subscriptions, and before long, Wally's multiple-title magazine-publishing business was in trouble. He eventually had to shut them all down and joined the ranks of the unemployed. Married for five years, in 1930 Wally and Marion were forced to pack up all their belongings and find a new place to live. Wally had worked ranches in his younger days and, figuring there was always a need for cattlemen and sheep herders, decided he and Marion should move to Oregon and start all over.

The couple still had Wally's teardrop trailer and initially thought they could use it to make the trip to Oregon. It would save them the cost of renting rooms along the way and would give them a place to stay once they got there, at least until they found an apartment.

The Airstream Clipper was one of the most luxurious camper trailers of its time, and boasted an advanced aluminum body for lightness, and aerodynamic styling so it could slip through the air.

The Wisdom of Owning an Airstream

Within the collector-car hobby, there's an old saying about Rolls-Royce automobiles that can also be used to describe Airstream: "Old Airstreams never become used trailers, they become classics." Don't believe it? Try pricing out a 1950s Airstream in good condition.

ADVENTURE IS YOUR COMPANION IN AN AIRSTREAM! Wherever you venture... via the twinkling Paris boulevards... the inviting beaches splashed with color and laughter along the sunny Riviera... and through every friendly little picturesque village along the way ...fun and high spirits ride with you. Excitement seems to dash ahead in order to join you at your next unscheduled stop. As commander of your own Land Yacht, your mood is your only itinerary. You'll never think of reservations or hotel prices. Just glance in your rear view mirror to remind yourself that your handsome craft is following with every comfort: Comfortable beds, heat, lights, hot and cold running water, a complete bathroom... all independent of outside sources. Inspect the completely self-contained Land Yacht at your Airstream dealer right away. Then go... do... live! Don't delay, for life is a one-time thing... enjoy it!

Traveling overseas with your vintage camper trailer can be expensive, mostly due to the cost of shipping the trailer to your destination and back, but your housing costs while there will be much lower than staying in hotels. And you can spend more time enjoying Europe while there!

The smallest aluminum Airstream trailers were usually called the Bambi or, later, the Sport. They were placed on a single axle. This one (perhaps somewhat improbably) is being towed by a Jaguar E-Type.

But before they even set out, that homebuilt trailer created an opportunity for Wally to earn a living even in the midst of the Depression. As the story goes, his handsome little trailer design attracted a lot of attention wherever the couple went, and at some point, a neighbor asked Wally if he would build him a trailer just like it. Anxious to make a buck, Wally agreed. After he and a hired carpenter quickly built a new trailer in his backyard, a funny thing happened. "It was no sooner finished when the fellow next door wanted one," Wally later recalled. Soon after that yet another person wanted him to build a trailer. Before long, Wally "began to think that this might be a pretty good business to get into." He and his hired man went to work on building still more trailers. They were busy as bees, but apparently made a little too much noise. Before long neighbors began complaining. Forced to move his assembly operation, Wally found a small commercial building for rent nearby where he could build his trailers in peace.

Wally Byam was now a full-fledged trailer manufacturer. Opening a new manufacturing plant—albeit a small one—at the beginning of the Great Depression was very much swimming against the current, but Wally was completely unfazed. He knew his strengths and weaknesses and decided to create his own luck. It turned out that trailer manufacturing was one of the very few growth businesses during the Great Depression. People were moving around the country in search of work or opportunity, so Wally's company got off to a good start. His first factory was situated on Motor Avenue in Culver City, California, but in time that facility proved too small for the growing business and Wally relocated to a larger building at 22nd and Grand Street in Los Angeles. In deciding what to brand his small, wooden teardrop-shape trailers, Wally decided to call them "Airstreams" because they were so aerodynamic that they traveled down the road "like a stream of air," he claimed. "Streamlining is Clean-lining" he added.

THE FIRST FACTORY-BUILT AIRSTREAM

The first Airstream model Wally offered was a plywood trailer called the Airstream Torpedo Car Cruiser. In this debut model Wally introduced a new, lower floor that he created by building the floor between the frame rails rather than atop them. His idea was quite an innovation, providing greater headroom inside while allowing for a lower, more aerodynamic exterior height. "This was a real milestone," Wally recalled. "We were able to install a table with an inset wash basin, a gasoline stove for cooking . . . and even an icebox, in addition to a bed." It also set the tone for Airstream as an innovative, pioneering company. In time the rest of the travel trailer industry would copy many of Byam's innovations. However when it came to innovations, Airstream always seemed to stay ahead of the pack. Byam was a dyed-in-the-wool camper who knew what fellow campers wanted in their vehicles.

Other folks like to take their Airstream trailer out on the open road, traveling to see new places and enjoy new experiences.

The Best Club for Airstream Owners

Although there are many good camper trailer clubs, owners of vintage Airstream trailers will feel most at home in the Vintage Airstream Club (VAC), an intraclub of the Wally Byam Caravan Club International (WBCCI), the largest club devoted to Airstream owners. The website for the Vintage Airstream Club (www.vintageairstreamclub.com) is loaded with information, including a history of Airstream, membership info, and a list of upcoming rallies and other get-togethers. Uncertain you qualify for membership? Here are the qualifications: Is your recreational vehicle made by Airstream and is it twenty-five years or older? If you can answer yes to both questions, you qualify for membership in the VAC.

The Airstream rallies are something to see, as hundreds of Airstream trailer owners gather for communal enjoyment of their hobby and swap tales with other club members. Joining a camper club is a smart thing to do, especially for newcomers to the hobby.

A beautiful 1966 Ford Thunderbird tows an equally beautiful vintage Airstream to some exciting destination. Although a single-axle trailer, this Airstream is a medium-sized unit with plenty of interior space.

This Airstream camper features plenty of modern stainless steel as well as deco–inspired curved wood.

By 1932 Wally's company was in full-production mode, after initially building Airstream trailers on a part-time basis. The unusual thing was that it seemed the more difficult the economy got, the better things got for Wally's business. Tens of thousands of families had been forced to move from their homes in search of work, and once they landed in whatever town they were headed for, they needed a place to stay. A trailer solved the problem of sleeping accommodations while allowing a freedom of movement that most people had never experienced. With a properly designed travel trailer a man and his family could follow farm work through the growing seasons and always have a comfortable place to stay. And, of course, every trailer owner realized that if their luck ran out and they couldn't find work, at least their family would have a roof over their heads that could move to wherever opportunity led them. A travel trailer was much less expensive to purchase than a one-family home, of course, so more people could afford them. Many folks decided to live in a trailer year-round, using it as their permanent address, though that was something Wally disapproved of—he felt that a camper should be used for camping.

At the time there was also a large market for trailers built for traveling salesmen. In these units one part of the trailer served as a home away from home, with a comfy bed, a sink for shaving, electric lighting, a work desk, and perhaps a radio for entertainment. This saved the salesman the not-so-inconsiderable cost of renting hotel rooms. The other part of the trailer housed a small showroom from which a salesman could show his merchandise to prospective clients. The trailer also had ample storage for his wares and personal

An American family, circa 1963, visits the historic Netherlands.

belongings. With such a unit, a salesman could stay on the road longer, for less money, seeing more clients than ever before. These special units proved especially popular.

What set the Airstream company apart from its competitors was that Wally Byam was a longtime, ardent outdoorsman who loved trailer living. Wally caught the camping bug as a youngster and never outgrew it. "Keep your eyes on the stars and the stars in your eyes," he once suggested, "and see if you can find out what's over the next hill . . . and the next one after that." As Airstream's owner, manager, and chief product tester, he made plenty of trips in the trailers to make sure they would stand up to any sort of punishment his customers might run into. Wally was his own test driver, his own product designer, and head of the product development team—and he loved it. Adventure, according to Wally, "is where you find it. Anyplace; every place. Except at home in the rocking chair."

Wally's business grew rapidly. By mid-1932 there reportedly were more than 1,000 Airstream Torpedoes on the road, with production continuing to ramp upward. In 1934 Wally introduced a second Airstream model, the Silver Bullet, which was a lighter trailer made with wood framing and Masonite body sides to reduce weight. This lightweight construction made the Silver Bullet much easier to tow even though it was wider than the Torpedo, which in turn helped provide interior space sufficient to fit a sideways double bed within its commodious confines.

Then in 1936 came the debut of an all-new trailer design called the Airstream Silver Cloud, the most luxurious Airstream to date and probably the most luxurious travel trailer on the road, with quality interior fittings and trim that rivaled the best hotels. The kitchen galley featured a three-burner stove, a sink with hand pump, and a lightweight wooden icebox, along with stylish countertops. The rest of the interior boasted fancy curtains, premium hardware, and silver and blue leatherette upholstery for a plush, luxurious look. With the Airstream Silver Cloud, Wally was consciously moving upmarket, which would end up being an especially fortuitous move by the time he made the decision to produce his trademark aluminum trailers. He wanted Airstreams to be recognized as the best in the business. Silver Clouds are rarely seen today and are highly prized by collectors.

BIRTH OF THE CLASSIC AIRSTREAM

To earn a little extra money, Wally took a part-time job selling travel trailers at a local dealership that sold the Bowlus-Teller brand of camp trailers. The founders of Bowlus-Teller were the famous aeronautical engineer and pilot William Hawley Bowlus and his partner Jacob Teller. Some years earlier Bolus lived by himself out in the California desert while conducting experiments on gliders. For living accommodations, he had designed and constructed an all-aluminum house trailer. His use of aircraft design techniques and aircraft-grade aluminum was a natural for an aircraft engineer, as was his use of advanced construction techniques. Realizing he had created a product that was years ahead of the rest, he went

Because of the weight of the larger Airstreams, they were built on dual-axle chassis. The dual wheels also offered greater trailer control in high winds and curvy roads. This one appears to be a team trailer at the Bonneville Salt Flats near Wendover, Nevada.

A 1936 Airstream Clipper with its body polished to a high shine, towed by an equally advanced-design Lincoln Zephyr, makes for an exciting scene. Note that both car and camper wear fender shields to lend an extra aerodynamic touch.

into business building aluminum travel trailers. With an exterior made entirely out of Duraluminum, (an alloy of aluminum, copper, and magnesium), the Bolus-Teller trailer featured innovative monocoque construction for the lightest possible weight with exceptional strength. Bowlus's Duraluminum body and framing was as strong as steel but weighed about one-third as much. At the time, most travel trailers were constructed with plywood or Masonite bodies over heavy wood framing.

The new Bowlus-Teller trailers were so superior, they should have set the trailer industry on fire. However Bowlus-Teller was unable to make a go of it, mainly because they were undercapitalized. Within a year, the nascent firm was bankrupt, with all its assets sold off at a bankruptcy auction in Los Angeles. Byam purchased those assets, which included the expensive tooling, a large inventory of materials, and rights to the trailer's design. The landmark Bowlus-Teller trailer would become the basis for a new premium Airstream model.

With the purchase of the Bowlus-Teller design and equipment, the look and feel of what became the iconic silver slipstream appearance of the soon-to-be-classic Airstream trailer began to take shape. But first Wally was determined to improve upon it. First off he moved the entry door from the front to the side of the vehicle, which was the same placement used on his own trailers. Wally also installed lightweight Sea-Pak insulation in the dead space between the interior and exterior walls, creating a much quieter interior that stayed warmer in cool weather and cooler in warm weather.

He priced the new aluminum Airstream at a lofty $1,200 (for comparison's sake, a new Ford two-door sedan could be bought for $520 back then). The redesigned and renamed trailer was introduced in 1936 as the Airstream Clipper. Wally decided to build as much luxury into it as possible. It featured a steel-framed dinette that converted into a bed and also had fancy electric lights throughout the cabin. The Clipper boasted cedar-lined closets, an enclosed galley kitchen, and full ventilation along with dry-ice air conditioning at a time when few American homes were air conditioned. The sharp new Clipper even carried its own water supply, highly unusual for the time.

The Airstream Clipper created a sensation wherever it went. Despite its premium price tag, the company quickly compiled a tidy backlog of orders. As Airstream advertisements boasted, the new Clipper was "Sleek-dashing-svelte-daringly new, modern in the extreme. It is the ultimate picturization of the streamlined age, so perfect that at speeds above fifty miles an hour the car that tows it uses no more gasoline than it does without the trailer." Even Wally must have been surprised when the president of Mexico, Lazaro Cardenas, ordered a specially built 22-foot (6.7 m) Clipper for personal use.

So sleek and so modern was the Airstream Clipper that it still looks great today. In fact the family resemblance to today's modern Airstream is so strong that, at first glance, a 1937 Airstream could easily be mistaken for a 2020 Airstream. That's a level of design continuity rarely seen in a product created for the road. But that

As Airstream design progressed, the tail end became less pointy, allowing for additional room inside. A perfect home away from home.

classic styling is at the heart of Airstream's enduring attraction to buyers new and old. And it's one reason why vintage Airstreams are so highly prized today.

Throughout his career, Wally Byam elevated trailering to a level of luxury once thought impossible. Fancy interiors replaced the rustic simplicity of the earlier days when everything was hand-sawed and homemade-looking. Modern conveniences like sinks, stoves, electric lights, and radios were becoming common, at least in the more expensive lines. Yet for all its luxury, the Airstream Clipper (and other trailers of the day) still lacked one modern feature: an indoor flush toilet. People in the industry had tried to adapt plumbing features

The 1969 Airstream Quarantine Trailer

For the 1969 Apollo 11 mission, when America landed a man on the Moon for the first time, NASA officials were concerned that its astronauts might possibly carry "Moon germs" back to Earth. Although everyone believed that the Moon was an airless, "dead" sphere, what if it wasn't? What if tiny microbes somehow managed to survive on its surface? To be extra safe, the American space agency contacted Airstream to build a special trailer called the "Mobile Quarantine Facility." Designed with special seals, it allowed the space crew to be comfortably quarantined upon their return to Earth.

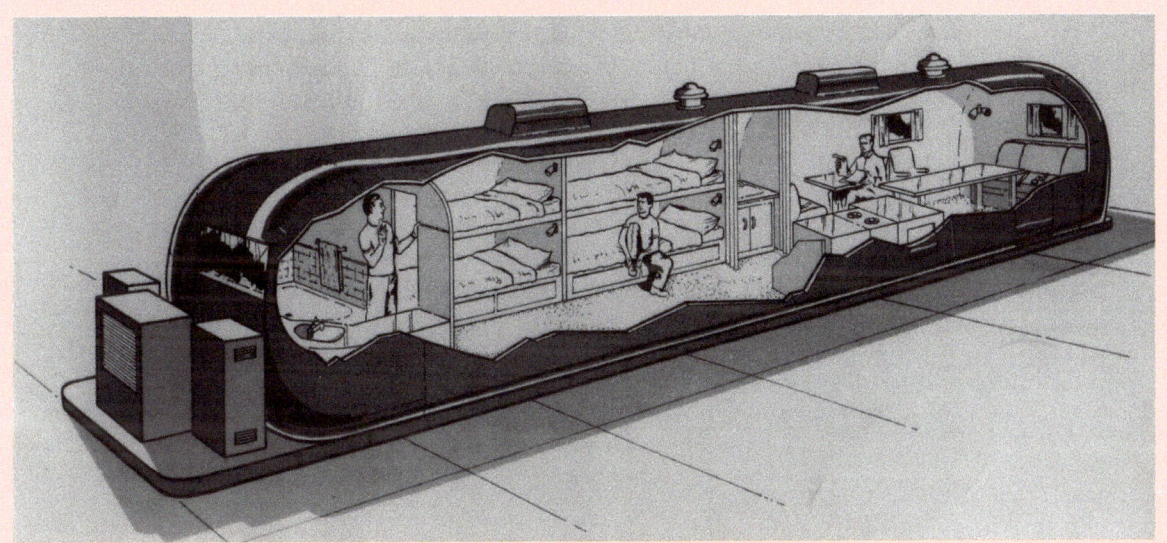

Built especially for the 1969 Apollo moon mission, this Airstream was designed to provide a quarantined home for the astronauts upon their return.

of boats into their trailers but, as Wally noted, nothing in the way of a toilet had been found to be transferable. Naturally the Airstream Clipper did offer sanitary facilities of a sort. One option was an old-fashion commode with a baked enamel finish for easier cleaning. Another choice was an airplane type "toilet" placed inside a small wooden box described as looking "like a cedar chest." Aftermarket outfits offered chemical toilets, but Wally didn't recommend them, noting, "The only difference between a chemical toilet and one without chemicals is that you just exchange one odor for another." A rustic by nature, Wally recommended the commode-type portable toilet, with a handy bail for easy emptying. He would empty it after every use, often into a small pit that he dug nearby. That was fine for him, but of course many found the whole idea of handling their waste completely embarrassing. Some trailer models offered a sit-down toilet situated inside the trailer but, lacking plumbing, simply emptied into a hole dug underneath the trailer—again, not a very elegant solution.

Eventually an engineer named Frank Sargent designed a real plumbing system for trailers. It came about when his wife, disgusted with the commodes then in use, told him if he was as smart an inventor as he thought he was he'd invent a real toilet and complete plumbing system for trailers. He did and in 1960 he brought the design to Airstream, which added it to its 1961 models. The days of digging holes in the ground to bury your waste were over at last.

During World War II Airstream went on hiatus. Although still in business, it built no trailers or any other products, for that matter. Byam took a job in the aircraft industry, making good use of his skills in aluminum forming and shaping to build planes and serve as a manufacturing instructor. He worked initially at Vultee Aircraft (which became Consolidated-Vultee in 1943), maker of rugged dive bombers, then moved to Lockheed, which built the incredible P-38 Lightning fighter plane. He later joined Curtiss-Wright Corporation where he was employed as a certified manufacturing engineer and production supervisor. Here his experience with Airstream really paid off, for Wally knew how to get things built. During 1943 he even taught a class at UCLA on aircraft fabrication and manufacturing methods.

The larger Airstream trailers are perfect for entertaining while on the road. Even in its original period furnishings, this Airstream still looks very inviting.

If you're thinking this photograph from 1967 is of a Florida vacation, you're wrong—it was taken in Hawaii! Imagine being able to spend weeks or even months in a remote paradise like this. The car is a 1967 Ford Country Squire, probably the most popular station wagon of the 1960s.

Part of Airstream's appeal is the large interior space and the extra nice fittings. This is a 1960s-era trailer—and look how much room they have for the family.

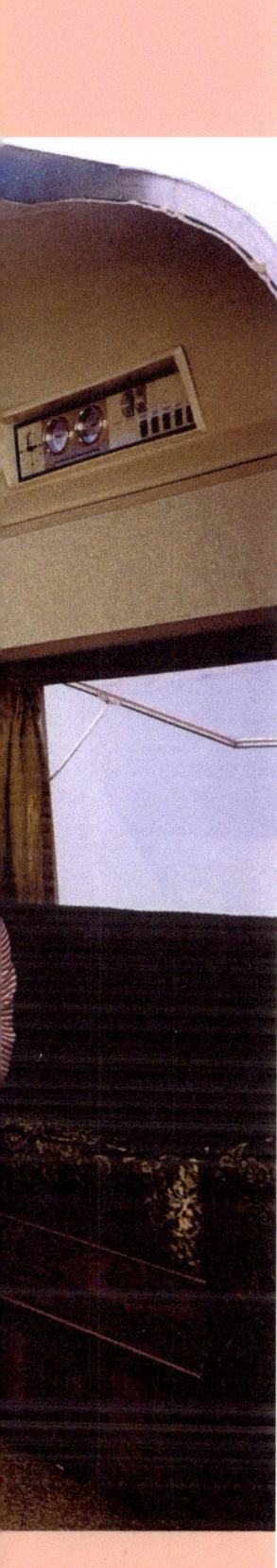

Wally worked steadily during the war years. When Japan finally surrendered in 1945, he was ready to get back to work on his Airstream trailers. He figured there would probably be a large, pent-up demand for trailers in the immediate postwar years. He was right.

But reviving his dormant company with the modern tools, dies, and equipment it was going to need would take a lot of money. To reduce costs Wally partnered with Curtis Wright (no relation to the aircraft company) to produce his trailers under the Curtis Wright brand name. Originally from Michigan, Wright had moved to California before the war and was looking for a business that would appeal to Americans' postwar desires. Like Wally he figured there would be a demand for travel trailers, so he teamed up with Byam to introduce a new trailer called the Curtis Wright Clipper. It was essentially the same product as the Airstream Clipper, but with as many improvements as Wally could incorporate. In time the Curtis Wright firm would introduce other new models: the Flagship and the Cruiser.

As soon as he could Wally opened his own manufacturing operation in a building at 1755 North Main Street where he set up a new business named Airstream Trailers Inc., which became a legal entity on November 1, 1948. Although it was a new firm in name and status, spiritually it was merely a continuation of the old company. Even after the long wartime hiatus and his reluctant partnership with Wright, Wally's principles had not changed, nor had his core beliefs. Everything prior to this in his life had merely been setting a stage for what was to become Airstream's future as a world-renowned maker of premium trailers built to an exacting standard and featuring timeless, iconic design. Wally was now ready to begin resurrecting his dream.

Growth was steady. By 1950 the company was solidly profitable and fifty-four-year-old Wally Byam was getting anxious to go out on the road. At an age when many men retire, Wally was loaded with energy and dreams. In many ways the 1950s would be the most exciting part of his life.

The company introduced a new Airstream model for 1951 called the Flying Cloud. It was a contemporary, handsome take on the classic Airstream design, a 21-footer (6.4 m) that featured a modern ladder frame, a unique A-frame tongue hitch, and front and rear caps that were flattened out a bit to improve interior space. Wally liked to brag that, like other Airstream trailers, the new Flying Cloud was manufactured on aircraft-style jigs, with aircraft construction techniques and aircraft-grade aluminum alloys. The Flying Cloud joined a growing lineup of Airstream trailers, including the 24-foot (7.3 m) Cruiser, 32-foot (9.8 m) Liner, and 18-foot (5.5 m) Clipper.

Wally Byam remained with Airstream until his death in 1962, overseeing the design of new models and making sure the company

Just as Airstream is the king of camper trailers, Jeep Wagoneer is the king of SUVs, and if you can match one with the other, you'll be in fine shape. Good hunting!

remained lean and customer focused. Today Airstream trailers of the 1950s and 1960s are some of the most collectible camper trailers on the market.

Airstreams of the 1970s and 1980s are very collectible too, but they don't have quite the vintage charm of the earlier models. However they do tend to be in better shape and thus need less restoration to make them serviceable. They also have more contemporary interior trim, if that's your thing, and more conveniences. Before buying any Airstream, check out models from several different eras to see which appeal to you the most.

This photo image came to us unidentified, but the trailer is an Airstream Bambi and the car is a Mercedes-Benz 190SL. Notice how much nicer the Airstream trailers look when they have their exterior skins polished to a high shine.

RECOMMENDED AIRSTREAM READING

Probably the two most comprehensive books written on the history of the Airstream company and its products are *Wanderlust: Airstream at 75*, published in 2005 and now out of print, and my own effort, *Airstream: America's World Traveler*, which is available at www.oldemilfordpress.com. Both books are high-quality hardcover volumes.

There are two magazines related to vintage Airstreams that you might want to check out too, both courtesy of the Vintage Airstream Club. *Vintage Advantage* was the VAC's own print magazine, published quarterly until 2013. The magazine featured articles written by vintage Airstream owners sharing their experiences. Also included were articles on restoration and repair. Although it's out of print, club members can view all copies online in the resources section of the VAC website.

Vintage Airstream Today is a bimonthly electronic newsletter designed to keep current VAC members informed of upcoming rallies and gatherings. It includes photos and written accounts of rallies, along with some very helpful technical articles of current restorations being undertaken by members.

The original glamper? This Airstream owner looks very comfortable, relaxing with a magazine in the sleeping area of her trailer. Notice how the seamless white interior walls accentuated available light. The effect brought the outdoors inside.

This cute little 1964 Airstream Bambi is perfectly matched to a similar vintage Ford Falcon compact sedan. The Bambi models were smaller units designed for smaller cars and budget-conscious families.

Cool Airstream Places to Visit

At **Kate's Lazy Desert Airstream Motel** you'll find six vintage Airstreams restored to offbeat perfection by talented artists and designers from across the country. Located in California's Mojave High Desert about twenty minutes from Joshua Tree National Park, there you'll experience incredible views, bright, starry nights, and the magical experience of sleeping in the desert.

Cape Town, South Africa, known as the "Mother City" of South Africa, boasts a variety of attractions, but one of the coolest is the **Grand Daddy Hotel**. The standard rooms are pretty nice, but if you're looking for a stay that you'll never forget, rent one of the rooftop Airstream trailers! To quote their website: "Take the Daddy's vintage elevator to our rooftop location in famous Long Street and soak in the alluring outline of the Table Mountains as reflected in the polished aluminum of one of our seven trailers. The seven authentic Airstream trailers all have their own individual décor theme and collectively reflect a typical South African 'road trip.'"

Caravan Outpost in Ojai, California, is a family favorite. The town of Ojai is a good place for camping in a fully decked out Airstream. Available trailers sleep one to five people and all come with record players and records, a good supply of books, and showers, refrigerators, pots and pans, plates and utensils—everything you need for camping. Air conditioning and heating are standard. At night, expect a bonfire and s'mores.

A 1969 Airstream towed by a 1969 Dodge Charger would be a really nice combination to own today. Notice the television antenna atop the trailer and the large picture window on the front end.

Argosy trailers are often called "the painted Airstream" because they look like an Airstream but are painted. The brand was created by Airstream in order to be able to offer a lower-priced alternative to its premium campers, but it's no longer being produced. There are still many of these out there and prices are much lower than that of an aluminum-skin Airstream.

Airstreams are the kings of the road, overall the most coveted of collectible vintage campers. Still a large number of enthusiasts prefer the styling of an old-fashioned teardrop trailer, a canned ham, or any of the stylish breadbox types. You need to go with your heart when deciding what style to buy.

A very popular pop-up brand was Skamper, which offered a full line of pop-up models from smallest to the biggest. Though there's no current listing for the company, some sources claim they were bought out by another RV company.

CHAPTER EIGHT

Pop-Up Trailers

———

Pop-up trailers are typically the second step in the progression that camper enthusiasts go through in the hobby, with tent camping coming first and a full-scale camper coming third. The way it usually goes is this: if someone who has experienced camping in the great outdoors decides to make it a part of their lives but wants to make it easier and more comfortable, they progress from sleeping on the ground in a small tent to sleeping inside a small pop-up trailer, where they can have the luxury of more comfortable beds, perhaps a small dinette, and usually even some indoor-cooking equipment. And all at a very affordable price. Not bad, eh? For many relatively new camping enthusiasts it's a proposition that's too attractive to ignore.

———

Got a 'wild' idea?

Live it... in a family-tailored Trade Winds camper

Big vinyl windows on our Continental let in the wild view, lock out any wild weather.

Ask your Trade Winds dealer to help you get that idea off the ground — with a camper family-fitted to your exact needs by a man who knows the score.

He may fit you into a Continental hard top. It will take you anywhere in the style and comfort you're accustomed to, because it's customized for you — giving you exactly what you want — no more and no less. Less a galley if you prefer to use cooking equipment you already own. More sleeping room if you want a second add-on wing. Wide choice of tailoring accessories enables you to camp your way — on the wild side or on the old camp ground.

Visit your dealer and inspect all the Trade Winds family-tailored campers (both hard and soft top models). All offer a basic combination of quality and travelability; color-coordinated interiors; stretch-out double beds with deep foam mattresses; easy up-and-down erection systems and quick-adjust leveling.

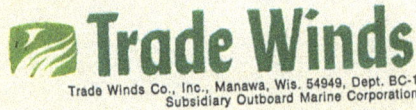

Trade Winds
Trade Winds Co., Inc., Manawa, Wis. 54949, Dept. BC-1
Subsidiary Outboard Marine Corporation

Trade Winds was a very popular brand of pop-up trailers for quite a while. A subsidiary of the now-defunct Outboard Marine Corporation, they were discontinued when OMC fell into financial distress.

Actually that natural line of progression also appears to be how the very first pop-up trailers were invented. In the early days of the automobile industry, between 1900 and 1925, family cars were usually small and very tight on cargo space, limiting the amount of stuff families could bring with them on vacation. So some people who enjoyed tent camping began hauling their tent and camp equipment in a small cargo trailer towed behind their car. At some point the campers realized they could actually sleep in the trailer, high off the cold wet ground; all they had to do was to erect a tent atop the trailer to provide the needed shelter (as mentioned earlier in this book, that's how Airstream founder Wally Byam got his start on the road to becoming a trailer manufacturer).

Exactly who was the first man or woman to build a tent trailer this way is lost to history, but in all likelihood several people reached the same conclusion in different parts of the country. Whatever the case, the idea caught on in a small way and in the period from 1900 to 1915, a handful of companies began to build commercial versions of "tent trailers" for sale to the public. These products were designed to fold down into the trailer while traveling to reduce wind buffeting, making it easier on the towing car.

Two early pop-up builders were the Detroit Trailer Company and the Campbell Folding Camping Trailer Company. The former was incorporated around 1913 to manufacture automobile and commercial trailers. Some historians consider them the first manufacturer of a tent trailer intended for camping and touring. It was very basic in design—essentially a flat trailer with a removable canvas top. Inside was a spring bed with room for storage underneath, plus an icebox mounted underneath at the rear.

In 1914 the Campbell Folding Camping Trailer Company took out a patent application for what they referred to as a "Combined Camping Outfit and Box." This appears to be the first patented folding-tent or pop-up trailer. The design was rather clever: the sides of the trailer dropped flat, creating a larger, level floor space on which rested the tent structure. It was basically an off-the-ground tent— you provided your own cot. The new tent trailers ended up creating demand for even better designs, and very soon entrepreneurs anxious to get in on the ground floor of a new and exciting industry began introducing new products. Between 1916 and 1919 new firms that introduced pop-ups included Auto Kamp Equipment, Continental Auto Parts, Cozy Trailer & Equipment, Curtis Trailer, Hercules Buggy

Camp Humor

Domestic Bliss
Want to know the best part about camping in a pop-up?
It's harder for relatives to drop in for a visit.

Works, Marx Trailer (which made the Komfy Kamping brand pop-up), Northway Trailercar, and many others.

By 1945 more companies had joined the industry, including Kansas City Trailer (maker of the Camp-Rite trailer), Klesa Tour-Home, Split Coach Motor (which produced pop-ups for Sears-Roebuck), Atlas Development (which made the Trailcar), and Trotwood Trailers, to name just a few. All are collectible brands—if you're lucky enough to find one!

By the 1950s and 1960s, the number of pop-up brands had dramatically increased even further, in line with soaring demand. Popular brands now included E-Z Kamper, Heilite Trailers, Higgins, Kamp Master (built by King Manufacturing), the Apache (built by Vesely Company), Kwik Kamp, the famous Nimrod pop-up (built

Seen here is a Ford Model A (produced 1928–1931) towing an early pop-up trailer of similar vintage. The man's clothing, however, seem to be of a more modern era, perhaps the 1970s? Think how great it would be to find a trailer like this in some barn.

Camp Humor

Steps to Building a Campfire
1. Split a dead tree limb into fragments and shave one fragment into small slivers.
2. Bandage left thumb.
3. Chop the remaining fragments into smaller fragments.
4. Bandage left foot.
5. Now make a small structure of the slivers, including those embedded in your hand.
6. Light a match.
7. Light another match.
8. Say to yourself, "I'm a happy camper" and light another match or two.
9. Now apply the match to slivers, add some wood fragments, and blow gently into base of flames.
10. Apply burn ointment to your nose.
11. Once the fire is burning well, collect some more wood.
12. Now add all remaining firewood.
13. After the unexpected rainstorm has passed, repeat the above steps. Apologize to all around you for your language.

This ad for the 1946 Karriall Kamper shows its clever design. A very low camper is set on a light, low-riding chassis but opens up to provide two comfortable beds and some room for sitting inside. Notice the handy storage in the side fender, and the tiny windows in the sleeping area.

Dating from the mid-1960s, this pop-up is of the larger family style, providing much more floor space inside with room for kitchen appliances, a table, and dinette seating.

by Ward Manufacturing), Sportsman's Trailers, and the Wayfarer (also built by Ward). The sharp little Apache remained in production until 1979 and there are thousands of used ones available, as well as a good supply of replacement parts. Sportsman and Ward Manufacturing both remain in business today, but neither currently builds pop-up trailers.

The 1960s saw a big uptick in the number of pop-up camper sales and manufacturers. Coachmen introduced its first pop-up in 1964. The first Coachmen RV products were manufactured in

This 1972 ad for the Apache trailer shows how elegant a pop-up can be if you buy the right one. This unit has a stove, sink, dinette area, plenty of storage and two sleeping bunks, as well as the dinette/bed.

Websites for Pop-Up Enthusiasts

If you've decided that a vintage pop-up trailer best suits your needs, the next step is to educate yourself on the best brands to collect and what to look for. A few websites can help:

www.popupcamperhistory.com This website is a good place to start if you're interested in learning more about pop-up campers and folding-tent trailers. Owners come together to exchange information, ideas, and tips.

www.canvasreplacements.com As mentioned earlier, Canvas Replacements is the place to go for replacement canvas for your vintage pop-up. Over the years, Canvas Replacements has expanded their line to include all major lift systems and, in 1991, they became the exclusive manufacturer of the only Universal Lift-Kit system for pop-ups. Their product range includes just about everything you need to enhance your camping experience, including a full line of awnings, mattresses, and cushions, as well as cleaning and care products.

This mid-size 1969 Trade Winds would make a nice vacation unit for any collector. Replacement canvas is easy to source, and the simple design means they're reasonably easy to restore to new condition.

Two outdoor vacation specialists are paired together in this 1970 advertisement—Jeep and Starcraft. The mid-size pop-up shown is a good size to look for because it offers at least some floor space and several sleeping options.

Coleman Products today offers an interesting line of camper trailers, but years ago it made a really nice line of pop-up campers. As seen here in this 1969 advertisement, Coleman offered the most basic type, as shown in the left rear of the picture, the most popular, forefront, and a terrific top-of-the-line pop-up, shown at the right rear.

a 5,000-square-foot (465 sq. m) plant in downtown Middlebury, Indiana, by Coachmen Industries, a company founded by three brothers: Tom, Keith, and Claude Corson. During Coachmen's first year in production they managed to build a total of twelve travel trailers, a single truck camper, and eighty truck caps. Things picked up in the decades after, and more than three quarters of a million Coachmen recreational vehicles have been produced. They're also a blue-chip brand: since 2008 Coachmen RV has been a proud part of Forest River, Inc., a Berkshire-Hathaway company.

Jayco, another company still in business today, began producing its classic pop-ups in 1969. Jayco remains a rock-solid brand that still makes pop-ups. Today they're a proud part of Thor Industries, the largest RV manufacturer in the world.

Good collectible brands to look for include Ranger, Starcraft, Apache, Jayco, Eagle, and Steury.

There are also retro-style pop-ups and A-frame units available from a variety of makers, but with the large supply of good used pop-ups at low prices, why buy new? It's a lot more fun to restore and enjoy a vintage pop-up than to simply buy a new one.

With two foldout beds—one on either end—plus a dinette that converts into a comfy double bed, even a small pop-up like this 1960s-era model can accommodate a family of five as shown here. Collecting vintage pop-up trailers is the easiest and least expensive way to get into the hobby.

The Joke That Started a Company

In 1954 Clyde Grambsch of Loyal, Wisconsin, designed and built a very nice pop-up camper for use by his family on vacation trips. He incorporated some unique features including a screen door and entryway steps (both unusual features in 1954). Two years after it was built Clyde had the camper repainted to match a new 1956 Ford he'd bought. As a joke, the painter printed the words "Mfg. by Loyal Trailer Co., Loyal, Wis." under the taillight. After the Grambsch family's next camping trip a few weeks later, the Loyal, Wisconsin, post office began receiving inquiries addressed to the Loyal Trailer Co. When Grambsch found out about that, he realized his innovative trailer had a strong appeal with the public, so in the fall of 1957, he founded his own company to build them, calling it E-Z Kamper. (Why he didn't call it the Loyal Trailer Company is lost to history.) The company built pop-up trailers until 1973 when Grambsch bought out his partners and refocused the company. Now known as Camper and Recreation Canvas Replacements, it is the world's largest supplier of replacement canvas for pop-up trailers of all brands.

When you're away from an electrical outlet, you want to make sure you have a good lantern and plenty of batteries. A battery-powered TV is always nice, and a hand-cranked radio is a must. And for goodness sake, bring a portable cellphone charger too!

WHAT TO BRING

When vacationing in a pop-up trailer, interior space is at a premium, so pack wisely. Ask yourself how much you think you're going to use each item you bring and if the answer isn't "a lot," leave it home. One excellent idea is to bring along an extra room to set up next to your trailer. This can be simple, like a 10- by 10-foot (3 by 3 m) pop-up shelter that you can relax under during the day. You can buy these for as cheap as $60, plus they don't take up much room in the trunk, and they're lightweight. You can pay a little more for a pop-up shelter with sides on it to give you more privacy and extra protection from the sun and bugs. Or buy a 12- by 12-foot (3.5 by 3.5 m) or larger wall tent to provide an extra bedroom, giving adults the privacy they sometimes crave. A decent tent can run you anywhere from $500 to $1,500 (or more), but the chance for some extra peace and quiet might just be worth it.

The Apache trailers are especially nice because they feature hard walls, a hard roof, and a full-size entry door. The crank-out system for setting up the trailer is illustrated in this 1973 advertisement.

ACKNOWLEDGMENTS

I'd like to thank my nephew David Foster for his help and suggestions, as well as my good friends Ray and Betty Hoffbauer, a couple of "campers extraordinaire." Jay Cowperthwaite also deserves a mention because over the years he's helped to educate me on the mechanics and culture of camping.

ABOUT THE AUTHOR

One of America's best-known automotive journalists, Patrick R. Foster is a dedicated historian/author who has been writing about cars for more than 25 years. Foster is a feature writer and columnist with *Hemmings Classic Car* and *Old Cars* magazines and is a feature writer for *Collectible Automobile*. He has written thirty-one books and contributed material to several others.

In 2011 Foster was honored with the Lee Iacocca Award, one of the most coveted awards in automotive journalism, for excellence in writing. The 2015 International Automotive Media Council (IAMC) Awards saw him bring home a silver medal for an article on the 1930–1934 Nash automobiles, and a bronze medal for his book *Jeep: The History of America's Greatest Vehicle*. In 2016 Foster took home two awards from the IAMC event when *International Harvester Trucks: The Complete History* won a silver medal and an article on George Romney was award a bronze. In 2017 Foster earned three more awards: the trophy for Best Book of Automotive History of the year for his *Airstream: America's World Traveler* (also a gold medal in its category) and a gold medal for *Willys-Overland Illustrated History*.

Born in Burlington, Vermont, Foster resides in Milford, Connecticut.

IMAGE CREDITS

B = bottom, L = left, R= right, T = top

Alamy Stock Photos: 24T, John Crowe; 27, Pamela Adler; 28, Jennifer Wright; 34, Zoonar GmbH; 35, BiR Photos/Stockimo; 37, John Crum; 47R, Andy Dean Photography; 84, R Kawka; 85, cmtransport; 86T, Michael Wheatley; 88, Matthew Richardson; 89, Richard Sheppard; 90, Justin Kase z12z; 91, Matthew Richardson; 92, Tracey Whitefoot; 93, imageBROKER; 99T, iWebbtravel; 100, David Askham; 102, Shaun Finch/Coyote-Photography.co.uk; 111, Gado Images; 112, Hum Images; 124, jonathan tennant. **Author Collection:** 8; 9L; 9R; 11; 12; 13B; 14B; 17; 18; 23; 24B; 26L; 26R; 31T; 31B; 32; 41; 42; 43T; 44; 49;47L; 54; 55; 57; 59; 60; 64; 66; 67; 68B; 70; 71; 72; 73; 74; 75; 77; 78; 79; 80; 81; 86BL; 86BR; 94; 95; 96; 97; 99B; 103T; 103B; 106; 108; 109; 110; 113B; 117T; 120; 122; 123; 125; 126B; 128; 130; 133; 134; 135; 136; 138; 139; 140; 141; 142; 143; 148; 151; 152B; 153L; 153R; 154; 157. **Creative Commons:** 6, PunkToad. **Getty Images:** 13T, William Vandivert/The LIFE Picture Collection; 15, H. Armstrong Roberts/Classic Stock; 20, Donovan Reese Photography; 21, Aladdin Color Inc; 25T, © CORBIS/Corbis via Getty Images; 36T, Douglas Keister; 36B, H. Armstrong Roberts/Classic Stock; 40, Alfred Eisenstaedt/The LIFE Picture Collection; 45, © CORBIS/Corbis via Getty Images; 46, Denice Breaux; 50, Berenice Abbott; 53, Speia Times/Universal Images Group; 62, Paul Popper/Popperfoto; 63, John Vachon/Anthony Potter Collection; 68T, Don Cravens/The LIFE Picture Collection; 76, Ralph Crane/The LIFE Picture Collection; 82, Sjoerd van der Wal; 98, Michal Fludra/NurPhoto via Getty Images; 101, WATFORD/Mirrorpix via Getty Images; 104, H. Armstrong Roberts/Classic Stock; 105, National Motor Museum/Heritage Images; 113T, Keith Beaty/Toronto Star via Getty Images; 114, Bettmann; 115, H. Armstrong Roberts/Classic Stock; 116L, Ralph Crane/The LIFE Picture Collection; 126T, Ralph Crane/The LIFE Picture Collection; 144–145, H. Armstrong Roberts/Classic Stock; 146, H. Armstrong Roberts/Classic Stock; 150, The Denver Post via Getty Images; 152T, H. Armstrong Roberts/Classic Stock; 155, Photo Media/Classic Stock; 156, Photo Media/Classic Stock. **iStock:** 3, adamkaz; 119, adamkaz. **Motorbooks Archive:** 1; 19; 25B; 38; 43B; 116R. **Shutterstock:** 4, Annette Shaff; 10, ampueroleonardo; 14T, chippix; 117B, Charles Harker; 127, Joseph Sohm; 129, Christophe KLEBERT; 132, Jeramey Lende.

INDEX

Airfloat, 39, 112
Airstream, 31, 40, 41, 42, 43, 44, 47, 56, 61, 120-145
    Bambi, 111, 124, 139, 141
    Clipper, 122, 130, 131-133, 137
    Flying Cloud, 137
    Mobile Quarantine Facility, 133
    plumbing in, 134
    Silver Bullet, 128
    Silver Cloud, 24, 128-129
    Sport, 124
    Torpedo Car Cruiser, 125, 128
Airstream: America's World Traveler (Foster), 140
Airstream Club, 116
Aladdin, 38, 47, 114
Alaskan Camper, 75
Alcoa, 42
Alma, 9
Amerigo, 79
Apache, 150, 152, 154, 157
Arcadia, Florida, 33
Argosy, 143
Aristocrat, 38
Arnaz, Desi, 117
Association of Cycle Campers, 101
Atlas Development, 150
Austin, 99
    Mini, 101
Auto Kamp Equipment, 149
Auto-Kamp Trailers, 14
Automotive Service Incorporated (ASI), 90
Avalon, 38

Baker, Samuel White, 98
Ball, Lucille, 117
Banjo on My Knee, 42
Bee-Line, 114
Benroy, 42
Boles-Aero, 38
Bone, Forrest and Jeri, 33
Bowlus, William Hawley, 129
Bowlus Road Chief, 31
Bowlus-Teller, 129, 131
Brahma, 69
Bristol Wagon & Carriage Works, 101
Burroughs, John, 16, 22
Byam, Marion, 122
Byam, Wally, 56, 122, 124-125, 127-129, 131-133, 134, 137-138

Camay Soap, 59
Camp Dearborn, 33
Camp Mate, 70
Campbell Folding Camping Trailer Company, 149
Camper and Recreation Canvas Replacements, 155
Camper Concierge, The, 21

camper shells, 66, 69-71
camper trailers, 47
Campermobile, 73
camping, definition of, 16
Camping and Caravanning Club, The, 101
Camp-Rite, 150
Campway's, 69
canned hams, 34-40
cannedhamtrailers.com, 34
Canvas Replacements, 153
Caravan Outpost, 142
Cardenas, Lazaro, 131
Cardinal, 38
CH Camper, 48
Chevrolet, 109
    Cameo, 69
Chicken War, 87
Chinook, 79
Citroen, 82
Coachmen, 79, 152, 154
Coleman Products, 154
Comet, 38
Conestoga wagons, 52, 56
Continental Auto Parts, 149
Corson brothers, 154
Corvette, 38
Covered Wagon Company, 56-63
Covered Wagons, 54-55
covered wagons, 51-52
Cozy Trailer & Equipment, 149
Craigslist, 22
Cree, Howard, 75
Cree Truck Coach, 75
Crown, 38
Curtis Trailer, 149
Curtis Wright
    Clipper, 137
    Cruiser, 137
    Flagship, 137
Curtiss, Glenn, 16
Curtiss-Wright Corporation, 134

Dalton, 38
De Soto, 24
Delray Imperial, 79
Desoto Park, 30
Detroit Automobile Show, 58
Detroit Trailer Company, 149
Deville Vagabond, 38
Devon Motor Carriage, 87, 90
Dickens, Charles, 100
Dodge, 65, 70, 77, 79
    Charger, 142
Dormobile, 87
Duraluminum, 131

Eagle, 154
Edison, Thomas, 16, 22
El Dorado, 77

Elcar, 114
Europe, camping in, 98-104
Eurovette, 90
E-Z Kamper, 150, 155

Family Motor Coach Association, 108
Fan, 38
fifth-wheel trailers, 48-49
Firestone, Harvey, 16, 22
Fleetwood, 31, 79, 114
Ford
    Country Squire, 135
    Falcon, 141
    Model A, 42, 150
    Model T, 14, 65, 122
    Super Camper Special, 81
    Thunderbird, 126
    truck-mounted campers, 72
    V8 sedan, 59
Ford, Henry, 16, 22, 65
Forest River, Inc., 154
Forester, 38
four-wheel drive, 80
Franklin Coach Company, 72
Franklin Silver Leaf, 72

Gemtop, 69
Gentleman Gypsy, The (Stables), 101
glamping, definition of, 16, 19
Glamping Hub, 19
Globetrotter, 111
GMC, 68, 75
Go Tag-A-Long, 114
Goldstar, 79
Good Sam Club, 111
Grambsch, Clyde, 155
Grand Daddy Hotel, 142
Grant, Ulysses S., 15
Great American Country, 21
Great Depression, 33, 56, 58, 122, 124
Gypsy, 38

Hallmark Campers, 75
Hanson, 38
Happier Camper, 48
Haynes, 114
Heilite Trailers, 150
Hemmings Motor News, 22
Hercules Buggy Works, 149-150
Higgins, 150
Highway Cruiser, 66-67
Holding, Thomas Hiram, 101
Holiday House, 113
    Model 19, 6
Hudson Super 6, 11

Illustrated Field Guide to Vintage Trailers, The, 118
International Harvester, 65
    Golden Anniversary, 69

Jaguar E Type, 124
Jayco, 154
Jayco Travel Club, 112
Jeep, 153
    CJ-5, 78-79
    Gladiator, 64, 74, 80
    Wagoneer, 138
Jubilee, 38

Kabin Koach, 12
Kaiser Jeep Corporation, 78
Kamp Master, 42, 150
Kansas City Trailer, 150
Karriall Kamper, 151
Kate's Lazy Desert Airstream Motel, 142
Kellogg, Charles, 73
Kenskill, 23, 38, 47
King, Walter, 75
King Manufacturing, 150
Kit, 114
Klesa Tour-Home, 150
Knight, 79
Komfy Kamping, 150
Kuralt, Charles, 22
Kwik Kamp, 150

Lacitinola, Paul and Caroline, 118
Lakewood, 38
Lance, 79
Land Rover Discovery, 103
Leer, 69
Lincoln Zephyr, 25, 130
Little Book of Camper Van, The, 116, 118
Little Caesar, 38
Little Gem, 38, 114
Little Vintage Trailer, 21
Livin Lite Recreational Vehicles, 76
Lockheed, 134
Long, Long Trailer, The (Twiss), 117
Los Angeles Trailer Works, 14

"M" System, 114
Mackinac National Park, 15
Martin-Walter, 87
Marx Trailer, 150
May Renewal Gathering, 33
Mercedes-Benz 190SL, 139
Mercury, 38
Metzendorf, 36
"More We Get Together, The," 31

NASA, 133
Nash Motors Company, 73
    Ambassador, 42
    Quad, 73
    Travel Log, 73
National Park Service, 15
National Serro Scotty Organization, 108
Nimrod, 150
Northway Trailercar, 150

Old Curiosity Shop, The (Dickens), 100
Oldsmobile, 23
On the Road, 22
Organic Act (1916), 15
Outboard Marine Corporation, 148

Pacemaker, 60
Palace, 115
Pierce-Arrow Touring Landau, 14
pop-up trailers, 147-157
popupcamperhistory.com, 153
Price, 38
purchasing a camper, 22-23

rallies, 116
Ranger, 154
Redman New Moon, 117
renting a camper, 21
REO, 65
Riley, 102
Riverside RV, 47
Riviera, 90
Roadmaster, 47, 115
Roma caravans, 98
RV industry, 10

Sargent, Frank, 134
Sea-Pak insulation, 131
Sequoia National Park, 15
Serro Travel Trailers, 18
    Scotty, 34, 36, 108
Shasta, 27, 28, 34, 47, 48
Sherlock Holmes, 17
Sherman, Arthur, 58
Sherman Laboratories, 58
Shermanite, 58
showers, 37
Siesta, 38
Sisters on the Fly, 13
Skamper, 146
slide-in campers, 64, 66, 68, 72-79
Sloat, 68
Snugtop, 69
Spartan, 115
Split Coach Motor, 150
Sport King, 75
Sportsman's Trailers, 152
Stables, William Gordon, 101
Stanwyck, Barbara, 42
Starcraft, 74, 153, 154
Starflight, 79
Steury, 154
Stiftung AutoMuseum, 94
Stockland, 69
Studebaker, 65
    Champ, 66-67

Teller, Jacob, 129
tent-style camper covers, 70, 71
Terry, 26, 115
    Rambler, 38
Tin Can Tourists, 30-33
Trade Winds, 148, 153
Trailcar, 150

Trailer Life, 118
tramping, definition of, 16
Travel Lite, 79
Traveleze, 109
travois, 52-53
Trotwood Trailers, 150
Truck Camper Adventure, 81
truck-mounted campers, 64, 66-69
Twiss, Clinton and Marie, 117

Universal Life-Kit, 153

Vagabond (camper), 47, 115
Vagabonds, 22
Vesely Company, 150
Viking, 100
Vintage Advantage, 140
Vintage Airstream Club (VAC), 110, 111, 116, 126, 140
Vintage Airstream TODAY, 140
Vintage Camper Share, 21
Vintage Camper Trailer Rallies (Lacitinola and Lacitinola), 118
Vintage Camper Trailers (Lacitinola and Lacitinola), 118
Vintage Camper Trailers (website), 9, 118
vintage camping, popularity of, 9
Vintage Trailer, 118
Volkswagen
    Beetle, 84
    Bus, 83-95
    Campmobile, 94
    Deluxe Microbus, 89
    Eurovan, 98, 99
    Kombi, 87, 88-89
    Microbus, 89
    Panel Van, 88
    Type 2, 84-86, 90-93
    Vanagon, 95-98
Vultee Aircraft, 134
VW Camper and Bus, 105

W200 Camper Special, 77
Wally Byam Camper Club International (WBCCI), 110, 111, 126
Wanderer, 101
Wanderlust: Airstream at 75, 140
Ward Manufacturing, 152
Wayfarer, 152
Westfalia-Werke, 87
Westwood, 47
Wheel Camper Corporation, 26
White, JP, 87
Willys-Overland, 65
Winchester, 102
Winnebago, 38, 47
wooden teardrops, 41-46
World War II, 61-62, 134, 137
Wright, Curtis, 137

Yellowstone (camper), 38
Yellowstone National Park, 15
Yosemite National Park, 15

www.ingramcontent.com/pod-product-compliance
Lightning Source LLC
Chambersburg PA
CBHW061141230426
43663CB00028B/2998